5-10-23

For Susan,
    Great to get to SEE
you in Bakersfield

Drina

End Suicide & Homicide - And The Harm In Between

Dr. Drina Fried, Ed.D. Author, Speaker, Consultant, Coach, Artist

Special <u>FREE</u> Bonus Gift for You!

To help you achieve more success, there are **FREE BONUS RESOURCES FOR YOU** at:

www.FreeGiftFromDrina.com

- In-depth examples on how you can talk with friends, family, and acquaintances - to help them find a better way, when they are leaning towards harming themselves or hurting somebody else.

- 68 Slide Educational Tool to aid you.

What Others Are Saying About Dr. Drina Fried

"I am so proud and thankful that you are giving such a gift for others. You are an inspiration for them to also pass it on. You have found your place to serve others from your long experience and training. You are making a difference. Keep it going!"

- Weston Lyon, Author of 20+ Books & Founder of PlugAndPlayPublishing.com

"READ THIS BOOK… The value of learning Offensiveless Defense to save lives is equal to learning CPR to save lives. more than 38,000 people commit suicide yearly in the united states alone. you will be empowered to stop suicide. you'll know how to recognize the tell-tale signs and how to respond."

- Andrew Hangarter, Tony Robbins crew, Hampton beach club owner.

"Drina served as a leader... She demonstrated an intervention and I continue to use this intervention today."

- **Sharon Sullivan,** MA Ed., School Psychologist, Kern High School District

"Drina was great. she has made a major impact on my life, all for the better. thanks, k."

- **Private Client**

"Thank you - we are much better. Never would have made it without you, Dr. Fried."

- **Private Client**

"Many thanks, Dr. Fried, for all your help and encouragement."

- **Private Client**

"Dr. fried took on the tasks of testing new and existing clients....as well as counseling in periods of crisis. The students benefited…. I highly recommend Dr. Fried. She has a wealth of knowledge and experience that would benefit those in need."

- **Gayle Rock,** Program Specialist, North High School, Bakersfield, CA.

"You really embraced the project and I think it's extremely timely and needed. When you first told me of the 2 declarations, they were interesting, but they felt so much more profound in the interview (on TV with you and Judi Moreo) when you talked about your son and I saw that once it was a part of a belief system, it creates real protection."

- **Kathy Hangarter,** Small Business owner and mother

Motivate and Inspire Others!

Retail $14.95

Special Quantity Discounts

5-20 Books	$12.95
21-99 Books	$10.95
100-499 Books	$9.95
500-999 Books	$7.95
1,000+ Books	$5.95

To Place an Order Contact:

(702) 283-1795

www.EndSuicideAndHomicide.com

endsuicideandhomicide@endsuicideandhomicide.com

The Ideal Professional Speaker for Your Next Event!

Any organization or group that wants to fast-start their people to become "extraordinary," needs to hire Drina for a keynote speaking!

To Contact or Book Drina to Speak:

Drina Fried, Ed.D.

3111 Bel Air Dr. #16A

Las Vegas, NV 89109

(702) 283-1795

www.drinafried.com

Drinafried@drinafried.com

The Ideal Coach or Consultant for You!

If you're ready to overcome challenges, have major break-throughs and achieve higher levels, then you will love having Drina as your coach!

To Contact Drina:

(702) 283-1795

www.drinafried.com

Drinafried@drinafried.com

Dedication

It is with respect, admiration and sincere appreciation, that I dedicate this book to my amazing grandmother- author Taylor Caldwell, and wonderful son, Mark Fornasiero. Without you and the lessons you have taught me throughout my life, I would not have the blessing of being where I am today. Thank you from the bottom of my heart! I love you both, dearly.

Table of Contents

Introduction
A Message to You

Drina Fried was a reluctant author at first. Growing up, she had observed how hard her grandmother, novelist Taylor Caldwell, had worked at her craft. Later in her life she was encouraged by colleagues to put her information into book form. Since 2005 Drina's been on a mission to show you that only two rules- AND a phrase she coined, "Offensiveless Defense" - are absolutely necessary for a safe and great life.

Preventing hardship, anger, and sadness that suicide and homicide brings to families and schools is the beginning. After 32 years as a school psychologist, Drina brings these strategies to more people, so you'll be trained away from psychological and physical harmful actions. You'll notice them more and commit yourself and others toward a life of benefits instead. You are a teacher, father, mother, grandparent, counselor, friend, lover, partner, student, sister, brother, acquaintance– you are in many roles of life.

Once you teach the method of offensiveless defense, through their demeanor those you teach will not even be targets of bullies. Sadly, some children are more afraid of their parents than they are of suicide. However, by using these methods, children will appreciate their elders so much that they will be open to talk about anything that concerns them.

Named School Psychologist of the year in Kern County, California, she brought her unique perspectives to teachers and parents so they would feel confident and ready, when confronted with these stressful situations.

Soon YOU will have that ability too, to turn others' thinking around, to get on track, living life the way it was meant to be lived, with delight and possibilities. Carry on!

Chapter 1
For Whom is this Book?
Suicide & Homicide
Statistics

You're still alive, so this book is for YOU! Tragically, it's impossible for this book to be for those 38,000+ people each year who committed suicide in the USA alone. Suicide is important to prevent. There are even more suicides than car accident deaths in the U.S.A. each year.

Learn these skills so you'll be ready. It's likely that you know at least one person, probably more who have or will contemplate suicide, or assault. If not now, you'll meet them in the future. It even might be you!

What will you say to them or to yourself to prevent that? How to get them (or you) back on track without letting yourself be harmed as well? Imagine how good you'll feel if you prevent a suicide or homicide. So please prepare here.

In case you think you shouldn't intervene, that it's "none of your business" or isn't your place, here's what the CDC (Centers for Disease Control and Prevention) says:

> "Many factors can increase the risk for suicide or protect against it.... For example, people who have experienced violence, including child abuse, bullying, or sexual violence have a higher suicide risk.... Suicide can be prevented. Suicide is preventable and everyone has a role to play to save lives and create healthy and strong individuals, families, and communities...."

> *https://cdc.gov/suicide/facts/index.html*

You are a teacher, parent, grandparent, counselor, spouse, friend, lover, partner, student, sibling, aunt, uncle, cousin, co-worker, – you are in many roles of life.

The future contains choices in which YOU can prepare to have a positive effect. Start by knowing some suicide and homicide past statistics. You can't change any of the past of course.

Suicide and Homicide Statistics

Suicides in USA in year 2020*	Homicides in USA
12.2 million contemplated committing suicide	1.2 million ER visits for assault **
3.2 million made a suicide plan	
1.2 million attempted suicides	Firearm homicides: 19,384 (2020)
Nearly 46,000 people died by suicide in 2020	Total Number of Homicide deaths***: 24,576

*CDC.Gov

**National Hospital Ambulatory Medical Care Survey- 2018

***National Vital Statistics System

- Mortality Data (2020) via CDC

Chapter 2
What's Blocking a Garden of Eden on Earth?

The answer to what's blocking a "Garden of Eden" on Earth is distress. I am passionate to show you how to get ready to prevent any current or future tragedy within your grasp. Stopping violence (outward harm), and stopping suicide (inward harm), is helped by understanding distress. So, you may choose to go forward to Chapter 12 which describes 4 methods of clearing out past negative emotions.

Starting with you: What about you?

Have you ever thought of committing suicide yourself?

Have you ever attempted suicide?

Have you ever felt like killing or harming someone else severely?

Have you ever lashed out, even to the slightest point of pain, either psychologically putting down someone's humanness, and/or physically to the point of pain, and beyond?

As a school psychologist in New York and in California for over 3 decades; and in private practice in California for about 29 years, I studied these problems each day. I tested, counseled, coached, and consulted with teachers, parents, individuals, couples, and groups to lead them away from hurting themselves and others, away from violence and suicide forever.

I can and will show you how to interrupt distress. These are ways to stop violence (outward harm), stop suicide (inward harm), by preventing big and small distress going forward. I am passionate to show you how to get ready to prevent any current or future tragedy within your grasp.

Chapter 3
Not Exactly the
Golden Rule

"The ultimate weakness of violence is that it is a descending
spiral, begetting the very thing it seeks to destroy."

-Martin Luther King, Jr.

Offensiveless Defense and the following of just two rules are
the only rules we may ever need for Bully Prevention, Suicide Prevention, Homicide Prevention, and much less need
for bereavement, grief, rage, and fear.

The problem is people (psychologically and/or physically)

a. hurting themselves as their (seemingly) last line of self-
defense.

b. hurting others as their (seemingly) last resort when
stressed out, because of outside factors.

c. The problem is not enough parents and teachers bring-
ing up their young people, yet, to accept and commit to
these two rules in their lives.

Simply put, the 2 rules are:

1. Never hurt yourself, neither emotionally nor physically.

2. Never hurt anybody else, neither emotionally nor physically.

Chapter 4
This Blueprint Starts with Yourself: Why Bother?

The Formula: Start with You:

1. Take an immutable (i.e., unbreakable) rule to never again hurt yourself; not physically and not psychologically. (e.g., even when you make a mistake, such as if you missed the turn on the road- don't call yourself "Stupid" and/or put down your humanness in any way. Say to yourself instead, "That's not like you. That's a mistake; focus to do better, Get back on track.")

2. Take an immutable rule to never again harm anybody else purposely. (e.g., when someone makes a mistake, don't call them "Stupid", and/or put down their humanness in any way. – kindly say instead, "That's a mistake. Get back on track. You're better than that. "(Or) - offer them some help to get back on track.

So, start with a brand-new habit of self-talk by saying such as, "Since I have a rule against hurting myself, _____." (For example, "Since I have a rule against hurting myself, I'll stop calling myself names)"..... "Since I have a rule against hurting myself, suicide is out of the question!")

And regarding your self-talk about others,

"Since I have a rule against hurting anybody else, "_____." (for example, "Since I have a rule against hurting anybody, much as I'd like to bash them for X (making so much noise), Y(moving my keys), or Z(messing up the house), instead I'll say, "We have a problem. I have some ideas on how to agree on a better solution. Maybe you do too. When can we talk about that?" Now?"

When interacting with others directly, say: "I have a rule against hurting myself and hurting others too, so _____." For example, "I have a rule against hurting anybody, including myself, so as much as I'd like to belittle you now for (a) your political opinion, (b) your thoughts on a proper diet, (c) how you spend our money; (or d) your behavior last night when we were with our friends, I won't. The relationship is more important than issues.

Without consciously taking these 2 rules yourself, it's like walking across a bridge with no guardrails on moonless nights; you will fall off the bridge eventually. Analogically, on "dark" emotional days, without taking to heart, practicing, and keeping these two safety rules over time, you will likely seriously harm yourself and/or others. So now, claim these rules as your own. What about if someone is trying to harm you? The concept I've called offensiveless defense will then come into play, and will be presented in detail.

The relationship is more important than issues. Instead let's both express our feelings of (anger, fear, disappointment, [whatever you truly feel] without hurting each other and talk about finding a better solution. I care about you. At worst, maybe we'll end up just agreeing to disagree [on this issue])."

The answer to "Why Bother?" is because by hurting yourself and others, you'll only make yourself and others worse, NOT better.

Chapter 5
What Happens When You Harm Yourself?

Hurting yourself takes away (Chips away at) the real you, that is, who you were meant to be.

Many people have written books about their suicide attempts. For example, Joy Hibbins in *Suicide Crisis the Story* became a mental health patient after she "experienced a traumatic event in 2012 which triggered Post-Traumatic Stress Disorder, a descent into crisis and more than one suicide attempt." Her "book contains a very honest account of her experience of crisis and her disturbing experiences within mental health services." In her case since she was unable to find the right kind of help "she set about creating something which would have helped her, and which is now helping other people who are at risk of suicide" in the United Kingdom. www.suicidecrisis.co.uk

You too can help people you know. With this commitment system, you prevent them from ever having to experience being a mental health patient.

Each time you hurt yourself, your unconscious mind takes it as the truth, and tries to make it true. For example, if or when you first smoked, you started coughing- it's your body's signal for you to stop. You kept going anyway. When you probably found yourself with a lit cigarette in your mouth, not even remembering when you lit it, your unconscious mind had taken over, without you even realizing it, going along with what YOU decided to do. (Yes, hurting yourself with smoking is what you decided to do.)

Every time you hurt yourself, the "real" you gets buried a bit. Unless there was terrible brain damage, you were born to be flexible, creative, rational, intelligent, loving, and cooperative. Many see that as having genius potential. Would you agree? Yet every time you hurt yourself, distress gets in you and interferes with your flexible creative, rational, intelligent, loving, compassionate, and cooperative actions.

Instead of putting yourself down, for example, if you've misplaced your keys, instead of calling out such as "Idiot! Jerk!", try positive self-talk that will avoid the drama and instead aim toward a solution. This might be,

"Okay, I always put them back (on the dresser). Think! Where else could they be? I'm smart. I'll figure this out."

If you are continuing to do anything despite negative consequences, you are hurting yourself. What if you're hurting yourself physically, such as smoking, or abusing alcohol, don't kid yourself...if you are continuing to do something despite negative consequences, you ARE harming yourself. By taking the rule of not hurting yourself, those addictions no longer fit your identity. It's time for you to seek alternative enhancing behaviors because you've become aware. You know the difference! For example, if you vomited and got rashes every time you ate carrots, would you stop eating carrots? Expect so! It's just that some addictions seem impossible to tackle. But that's the addiction talking. Swat that away! Also, if you'll need help, help is available.

When I was smoking 2-3 packs of cigarettes daily and drinking any drink someone put in front of me, (while in my late twenties, up to my mid-thirties), it was THEN when I also took these two rules. Mmm! So, I kept my commitment. I saw in Prevention Magazine that one (regular sized) drink a day for a woman, and two (regular sized) drinks a day for a man is okay to prevent brain damage and self-harm. So, one drink or less per day has since been my way of operating. Now I rarely even remember to take that one drink. I've found even more healthful and enjoyable liquids. Alkaline water and green tea are my current usual favorites.

Quitting smoking was harder and took longer. Suffice it to write that I managed to stop smoking, thought I could have just one a year later, and was back smoking regularly in less than a couple of months. Again, ugh! I used my method of quitting again at age 37, and ever since then, "Not even one or I'll be hacking again, etc. Therefore, I've not taken even one puff since then, and the urge is completely gone, as I committed to never start again, I have no desire to lose my benefits from quitting. So glad I bothered to quit; can't imagine whether I'd be alive, dead, or "on my last legs" by now. It's now more than 40 years since I've smoked.

What this means for you is, know what you're doing, make a better plan if you'd still be harming yourself, and keep at it until success. Then it gets a lot easier.

Scott Mayer of "*In Fitness and in Health*" notes, "As of 2020, 45 million Americans take some sort of antidepressant.... And 33% of those folks have been using them for longer than five years." Patients of mine who told me they used antidepressants noted that it numbs their feelings, numbing their good feelings as well. Some worried about the side effects they see in advertisements.

Learning to stop hurting yourself through eliminating self-putdowns and harmful actions will reduce the amount of distress that gets in you. This enables you to make even more flexible creative, rational, intelligent, loving, and cooperative decisions and actions.

Chapter 6
What Happens When You Hurt Someone Else?

ARE you harming somebody if you slap, punch, or otherwise make contact?

You might look like you are, and you might be annoying. However, mostly only you AND the other person will know whether you have actually crossed the line into hurting. Humans know the difference. Thus, pillow fighting can be useful. It can release frustration safely, and it can be fun. Arranging a pillow fight among siblings isn't a bad idea IF all concerned first have a rule not to harm anybody.

So, take the rule now if you haven't already. AND ONCE YOU AGREE TO TAKE A RULE NOT TO HURT ANY-BODY, make it permanent; embrace it. Don't go back on it. Feel free to bash pillows instead until the urge to hurt another disappears. Do it long enough, and repeat the right words, I guarantee with certainty, your anger and frustrations" will disappear. You also might influence your friends and siblings to do the same.

Usually when you hurt somebody, they resent you. They'll often want to hurt you back similarly – psychologically and/ or physically. Some people will shut down and become worse people.

Is that reason enough not to harm them? What you've done is not inconsequential; you may have done some permanent damage to your relationship. Also, they may try to get back at you. Tell them, "I could punch you, you could punch me, we could hurt each other, yet (whatever started this situation) is still there". "Let's agree to disagree." Remember, I care about you. I even love you."

This philosophy is often a way to go forward too, or at least to put the conflict aside until new or better information shows up. Or:

"Will you please let me know if you'd ever like to talk about this some more?"

When I was a school psychologist, I was sent the rough High School boys because they got into fights. They were angry and wanted to prove they were right or demonstrate their self-importance. The only way they thought they could do this, was by bullying and name-calling others. Much to my surprise, many were trying to straighten out the other student. (Their victims were not receptive to this technique.)

After showing bullies the folly of physical fighting to improve others, teach them to ask simple questions, and then you listen to the bullies' answers. You will be getting them to think about what they wanted to accomplish. You'll bring them closer to finding a solution.

At first, ask the bully if they were upset with the person, or with the overall situation. "What makes you angry (about this or them)?" Depending on their answer, you could start with _(remind them of the reason they are in your office) _____. E.g., You were sent here because _____, and it disrupted the teacher, so s/he couldn't teach the lesson."

"It's not your fault, but has anybody in your life ever asked you to take a rule, from this moment forward, to never again hurt yourself and, never again hurt anyone else? (Wait for a yes or no.) That's when you begin the process of getting them to accept both rules for their own benefit.

Depending on their age and comprehension, tell them this story of walking across a bridge nightly with no moon to show them when they are at the edge.

> "If you walked across a bridge every night, and there was no moon to show you when you are at the edge, wouldn't you probably fall off some dark night? Maybe you would even die? However, with bridge guardrails to keep you

on track, you can't fall off. Same thing about having these two rules. With them, whenever you do feel scared, angry, sad, bored, or any of the bad feelings, hurting yourself or somebody else won't happen, because you've taken the cornerstone rules against it."

Go back and forth while listening carefully, having patience, and noting their feelings. It invariably happens sooner, by your starting with the rule of not hurting themselves:

Ask them to repeat after you and see how it feels to say: **I promise from this moment forward, to never again hurt myself, both psychologically and physically.**" *Ask them to again repeat the commitment while copying your assured tone of voice.*

If necessary, explain the difference between psychological (the science of mental life) and physical. Give examples of both bad thoughts (such as saying, "I hate myself" or "Good things never happen to me". That is keeping yourself down, so that is mind or mental damage). While punching a wall or allowing yourself to be reckless while riding a bike could damage your body; that's called hurting yourself physically.

When they know the difference, make the following analogy, in words they can understand. ("So, if you agree that you'd probably fall off the bridge one dark night if there were no guardrails on each side, would you also agree (in other respects) that when your mind is upset or when somebody else upsets you, with no guardrails or rules, you might harm yourself or someone else if you don't have a rule against harming yourself and harming somebody else? " (wait for them to think about it and answer "Yes, I might hurt myself or somebody else…. So then, ask them to repeat those two rules after you, perhaps for the last time; especially if you write it out for them to take from you.

1. *"Repeat after me:* **I promise to forever keep a rule against hurting myself, psychologically or physically. This will mean** _____" have them finish the sentence.

2. *"Repeat after me:* **I promise to forever keep a rule against harming anyone, psychologically or physically... Do you have any thoughts?** Tell them (later) you will (now) show them the magical method of offensiveless defense, based on research. Use it to block anyone from hurting you. (Then add) *"This will mean* _____" (have them finish the sentence.)

Chapter 7
Are You Harming Yourself or Another by Saying Goodbye?

No, you're not hurting yourself or another by saying good-bye if you're saying goodbye to a wrong or toxic relationship. They might feel sad, and you might feel sad too. That would be normal and appropriate.

You're likely not to be "right" for them if they are not right for you. This frees you both up in the long run, to look for a better situation. Best to kindly explain this to the other person, rather than to leave them wondering, to "ghost them", or to drag out a wrong relationship.

Chapter 8
Learning Spankings versus Damaging Spankings

Regarding spankings for young people: When you are irked by a young person in your charge- any physical contact might not be the best choice, unless you understand the difference between Learning Spankings and Damaging Spankings.

1. There are learning spankings

How can a parent or teacher use an uncomfortable moment to help a young person learn? Get their attention by using a spanking motion, with sound. If you decide to make contact, e.g., on their shoulder or arm (rather than on the table), keep the force **less than the point of pain**. Do this while speaking calmly, rationally, and making as relevant as possible suggestions to the young person.

One of hundreds of possible things you can say is, "When you daydream in class, bring your mind back to the lesson-taking notes is one way to help you focus. Any ideas of what else might work for you? This lesson may be very important for you someday, you never know, for a job or hobby in the future."

"When you (xxxx-exact details so they know the irking part), I get so angry that I want to bash you. But I won't because I don't want you to be hurt, dislike me, or to stop being cooperative". Besides, I have an important rule to not hurt others.... or myself.

Another example, "Smoking and drinking alcohol is asinine; YOU are not asinine." Call what they have done names, but **don't call them bad names**.

(Take time to think of proactive, redirected, or offensiveless defense responses such as.) "Walls are not for writing. Paper is for writing" "People are not for hitting! Hit here (e.g., Hold out a pillow) instead." "When you interrupt my class (my work, etc.) so much while I'm teaching, I lose my train of thought and I can't do my job well."

Attention is heightened with this type of touching-spanking, so learning can happen, and behavior can change. Keep it fairly short without too much repetition. This technique is very effective for getting their attention. Make sure you have a good lesson or point to impart.

2. There are damaging spankings

Damaging spankings are those that go into pain and any level of damage. Pay attention and you'll know the difference! They result in the person shutting down and becoming resentful. Damaging spankings impede learning, even if you are speaking calmly and making suggestions. Back off from using spankings that go into pain, as they result in stopping natural cooperation. Your relationship will get worse and worse by using painful spankings.

When you are irritated by a young person in your charge and are tempted to give pain- back away. Painful physical contact is a bad choice. Avoid touch altogether by diverting yourself:

Experiment with this recipe instead:

Wring a coat, twist a pillow, or bash a soft inanimate object several times, so they also get that you're not hurting yourself either. Even use a belt if one is handy. (I used a cane once - it could've been a stick) – You use it on a bed, the floor, or on a chair seat or couch, while saying, "If I didn't have a rule against hurting anybody, this might've been you" .... I guarantee that this can be interesting for the child, helping them turn away from immediate disruptive behavior, wanting to hear what you'll say. Give details as to what you find repulsive, and what you'd rather have happen in the future.

E.g., I hate it when you _____, because _____! Instead, I wish you would _____ (tell them what you want them to do _____. Not that they will, but you will have expressed yourself. (Maybe it's their loud music or constant messy area that bothers you...?) Perhaps by saying this you'll get rid of some your own anger and frustration, and they won't be harmed and feel resentful. End with "Let's find a better solution later.... unless you have a good idea now." (Listen for something useful and appreciate them when they come up with consideration for you, no matter how small.)

If you are interrupting THEM from harming themselves or somebody else, say it slightly differently. Keep the pillow wringing and/or bashing some soft inanimate object, or the belt or cane, and instead firmly say, "You're not going to (e.g., hurt yourself" (or) "hurt anybody else, such as your brother".

"Stop it! No! Do what I'm doing. Hurting yourself or anyone else is not acceptable (in this household!) (in this school)!"

If they seem angry, hold your coat or pillow out to them, and say, "Hit here instead! Try it. You'll feel relief after a little while. Especially you'll feel better if you say something encouraging or constructive to yourself (or to your sister). The positive thought or out-loud statement may not be true yet, but it has a better chance of going in a good direction over time." Ask them, "What's bothering you?" (or) Ask them to do something else instead. Maybe they will.

"Maybe you two can work it out. For now, just get your frustration out on the (pillow or couch). Okay?"

(Parent, Teacher) Reader: Can you do that? It may be uncomfortable to react like this the first few times. Yet if you can do that, if you can do it in the here and now, you will not have lost them. You'll be keeping your relationship(s) intact.

Chapter 9
Introducing the Offensive-less Defense Philosophy

First and Second Line of Strategies to Use for Offensiveless Defense

#1. First line of defense: TELL THEM WHAT THEY ARE DOING (once); "You're mocking me! "...or "That's mean" Repeat once EACH TIME THEY DO IT. E.g. "You're mocking me again! "..."That's still mean! ". ...

Walk away or shed a tear that they see, if it's real;

Later if/when they come to you:

#2. Second line of defense: WHEN THEY LOOK AT YOU AND SEEM TO WANT YOU TO SAY SOMETHING OR REPLY ...only then, TELL THEM HOW IT MADE YOU FEEL. E.g. "That makes me "sad," "angry" "disappointed" "frustrated" "embarrassed" (look at the feeling words in chapter 12 on the continuum "(FILL IN THE BLANK WITH A TRUE FEELING WORD; say it once. Repeat once EACH TIME THEY DO IT. E.g. "That really makes me feel "sad," "angry" "disappointed" "frustrated" "embarrassed" ""That made me feel sad at first, but then it makes me feel scared to be around you – (whatever it actually makes you feel -say just that. THAT'S ALL YOU NEED TO DO. If you want to get more complex and creative though, there are some suggestions for that. What if they say some form of "I don't care" ... THEN say "Okay, and I don't have to be around you anymore". Or "I don't have to be your friend though."

First, know that people rarely if ever improve with blame, reproach, and/or attack. You don't either.

If you feel yourself being emotionally (same as psychologically) hurt, somebody is usually blaming, reproaching, or verbally attacking you, It's the same with physical attack.

It often was how they were treated badly long ago, (or as they SAW somebody else poorly treated in similar situations.) They are passing it on, like a common cold. It's a way of responding they've come to believe is normal behavior.

You find the right words to let them know that it's not acceptable behavior and not in their best interest either. Your chosen response holds up reality to stop them. It stops their attack without attacking them at all. Using offensiveless defense is not the same as teaching others to use offensiveless defense. So, first use offensiveless defense yourself. (After you do that a few times, you are ready to show people you love how to use offensiveless defense too, to protect themselves.)

Getting ready to act and use offensiveless defense is rather similar to taking CPR training. You wondered if you'll ever need to use cardiac pulmonary resuscitation. CPR has saved many lives. You probably also wondered if you would be able to do it, under a stressful situation. You might also feel that way about using Offensiveless Defense. That's okay. As you know, many people have done CPR, in an emergency- in a clutch -, when needed. They started not knowing, they paid attention during the class, and even though uncomfortable at first, they managed when the time came. So can you.

So please pay attention to your thoughts and feelings, and how you express them to others. Which reminds me of a pet peeve of mine: I don't know if you do this, but MANY people do, and become confused about feelings versus thoughts. Usually they don't even realize that they call thoughts feelings. For example, you might say, *"I feel it's important to floss and brush your teeth before bed."* No! You don't feel it's important, you think *it's important (to floss and brush your teeth before bed).* You could say, *"I feel disappointed when you go to bed without first flossing and brushing your teeth....I think flossing and brushing your teeth are important.* Disappointed is a feeling. This will become most clear in Chapter 12 about clearing out past negative emotions to recover your creative, flexible, appropriate, and rational thinking. So, will you please notice, and correct yourself from now on when you say a thought but use a feeling word? It is so very important to communicate as well as possible, because it involves the quality of your life.

The purpose of using OFFENSIVELESS DEFENSE is to turn around a developing bad situation, and stop somebody from hurting you, without hurting them back. You are aiming to turn a negative situation into a neutral situation, and even potentially into a positive outcome.

It will need your flexible intelligence in each unique situation. You will do it without going offensive, without "tit for tat". Until it becomes natural for you, it might take all your wit and personality. However, it's worth it. Offensiveless defense is mostly a matter of responding from the heart truthfully, with the idea of then walking away, or carrying on, with everybody's self-esteem intact.

Don't let fear get in the way of protecting yourself. This is not a fight or flight situation. Keep thinking, and when ready, speak positively: Keep your eyes open, be in "present time", don't shutdown.

One example of offensiveless defense was shown in a Ron Howard movie, "Cinderella Man", near the end. Two boxers found themselves in the same restaurant. One boxer was relentlessly egging the other one on (Russell Crowe character) to fight. The wife, played by Renee Zellweger, intervenes by tossing a glass of water at him, and Max Baer sneers, "Now you got your wife fighting your battles!?" Instead of taking the bait, where the first punch would then be thrown, Russell Crowe instead says, "Yeah, isn't she something?"

Let me share another story that taught me how I might enlist someone else to help.

I asked my adult son to help me. I explained that every time I see my ex-brother-in-law, ("as we will be seeing him to-night"), he teases me to the point I don't want to be there. I put my head down and I go somewhere else in my mind. Last time it happened I tried to interrupt him. I told him that while he's having fun teasing, I'm not. I even told him that my favorite psychiatrist, deceased Haim Ginott, essentially said that teasing isn't a good way to relate to people. Dr. Ginott meant teasing's not a good way to relate to children. Yet some of us are generally sensitive, especially when it comes to feeling put- down.

I asked my son to make sure I'm not seated near his uncle, and I asked him to come up with something that will inter-fere with his uncle's irritating pattern of teasing.

That night, during predinner drinks, uncle starts in. My son kindly but firmly said, "*I don't think mom is in the mood for rib-bing.*" Boom! Done! End of story.

A few months later the brother-in law and his wife came to my city and wanted to get together. Never once did he tease me. The one sentence proclamation carried over into the later situation, and we got along better than ever.

Got it!? Whenever you are threatened or put down is the time to start thinking about using offensiveless defense. Start with the first and second lines of defense, or even be more creative. Perhaps also enlist the help of someone else to help you find the right sentence that doesn't inflict harm.

You explain to your helper that the principle of offensiveless defense means you're protecting yourself or somebody else, without lashing back. Then you explain the problem and ask---What can be said to them? Together you formulate best response, and one of you delivers it. Writing it down often helps—because you're likely to forget it---because offensiveless defense isn't second nature to you yet. You might alter it in the real situation a bit. Still, by reading it over enough, you'll be ready, and possibly even be thought of as a professional negotiator.

Often while consulting and coaching couples, I've found that they've misunderstood each other. Then out of frustration, they might cross the line into inflicting emotional, even physical, pain. It's downhill right there. Immediately say, *"Cancel Cancel! Let's back up!"* to before anyone crosses the line. (Apologize immediately if it's too late, due to any putdown or transgression.) Go to right before the (probable) misunderstanding and break the pattern: Be the one to say, *"I'm confused, what did you mean to say? I thought you said _____"* (listen).... Tell me more. (Listen more). So you think

_____. *Right?* (Listen and wait until they say *"Yes"*. Perhaps happily with celebration, say, *"I got it now!"*

I saw a person step up to two young people, *"You're not going to hurt each other."* One small adult, two large teenagers, looked at each other, turned around in opposite directions, and walked away.

Perhaps you can imagine sketchy situations you've seen in the movies, on the news, or in your environment. You may come up with something witty, something smart, using your own personality. E.g., You are bothered by hearing loud music coming from a neighbor's condo, late at night. Imagine yourself approaching their door.

You knock. Somebody answers. *"Hello?"* You: *"I hear lots of loud music. I can't sleep...* (wait while you count internally for 3-5 seconds). Slight smile: *"How come I wasn't invited?"*

Do you think you'll be glad to have and use offensiveless defense in your life? Rehearse doing it. It's a useful tool.

Chapter 10
Never Go Back on the Rules

If you already have these two rules -as unchangeable- for yourself, not hurting yourself or another- along with offensiveless defense, good! You have what you'll need for safety. YOU HAVE WHAT YOU NEED TO MANAGE MUCH STRESS. Without them your life will someday become unmanageable. Never go back on those rules. Take them "on faith" if necessary and see how your life goes. Taking rules not to hurt yourself and not to harm another can happen anytime! No harm by taking them "on faith".

You've already taken the rule against harming yourself, so focus instead on doing activities to improve your life and that may also raise your self-esteem. That will interrupt depressed and suicidal thoughts by getting you into a higher state of mind.

Here's the overall plan:

Search for endorphin production through having fun safely, by gaining feelings of freedom, gaining competence in one or two areas of interest, and by being closer to others. Daily make sure you are well-rested, well-nourished, well-exercised, and well-organized. Then schedule these activities.

All this translates to a myriad of example possibilities. Tailor these areas into specific examples for you. Put them on your calendar. Follow the plan to keep yourself moving. Go to a comedy movie, take a friend to lunch and see if you can understand and solve a problem of theirs, watch your niece play soccer, donate blood, compliment people on their gardens or about their clothing, take a slow walk in your neighborhood. Get up; move around; do the next indicated thing.

That will fill your days, and at some point, your purpose for living will also emerge. Think of yourself as trudging the road to healing and happiness.

Beware all the while of continuing to use or do anything in your life that results in negative consequences, which is a definition of addictions. Cut those out. There are so many other good things in life. I like to say you'll rarely miss it. You will actually appreciate your new habits even more.

I would've told all those things to one student who was sent to me, the one person in my 32 years of work who did commit suicide. It impacted me greatly. It still makes me so sad. Thinking back, it may be one of the reasons I'm writing this book. Let me tell you what happened.

It was rather early in my school psychology career. A student was referred to me. Near the end of our time together, she agreed to the rules that I presented of not hurting herself, and not to hurt others. It hadn't occurred to me in those earlier years to add, *"Are you willing to never go back on these rules?"* (Then I would've listened to anything she had to say.) Instead:

Her counselor told me months later, that she had asked to see me again. She was told that I was too busy testing students. She asked her teacher aide a question, *'I know it's not right to hurt anybody, but isn't what I do to myself my own business?'* Apparently, the teacher aide agreed. That evening she was said to take her father's gun and kill herself. No! Suicide is not a good or necessary choice. Just because somebody doesn't return your love doesn't mean you'll never have love in your life. That's what brought her to counseling in the first place. Deep disappointment over unrequited love. If I could've seen her again, I would have helped her dissipate and release more of her anger and sadness, as in "The Human Side Of Human Beings" by Harvey Jackins. Then we would have tailored a plan as I just asked you to make for yourself, and/or with your young people.

"Before we part, repeat after me, (make sure that she copied saying it in a confident tone of voice) *"I cheerfully promise to take two never changing rules; not to hurt myself and not to hurt anybody else!"*

What does this mean for you? Something very important. You can do it. Knowing what you know now, I bet you could've saved that girl's life. You still may save a life where you are now. You can also add the idea that they should call on you, or tell another adult that you said they can call on you anytime, if they feel overwhelmed like this again. Also there are many new suicide hotlines that exist, that didn't exist then. For example, 988; or 1-800-suicide.

Teach others, whenever and wherever you are, so those you care about, or just met, will be safe as well. They can take these two rules from you. You'll get closer to a heaven on earth when suicide is no longer on your table; and when you also forbid yourself from lashing out at others, such as "You piece of sh__.!"

In the meantime, do the work to get your life even better, so that you are prepared.

1. a) Plan more endorphin production through scheduling some fun.

b) Gain feelings of feeling free (For me feeling free was going for a meandering bicycle ride. My partner felt these feelings of freedom as he was getting off the school bus on the last day of school.) Recall at least once when YOU felt feelings of freedom.

c) Grow in competence on a topic that you've been curious about learning. It could be painting; it could be learning to play chess (better).

d) Become close to others. One way to get closer is by approaching others with questions to which you care to hear answers, AND that are about them. For example, *"What's new and good since I saw you last.* (name when and where)? This shows you're think about them. Always wait patiently for them to think and answer. You might follow up their answer with another question such as, *"What's the biggest little frustration in your life lately?* For people you just met, my coach James Malinchak, suggests asking the three I's: *What are your interests?* (Listen carefully.) *What's important to you in your life now?* (Listen carefully.) *Do you know what intrigues me about you?* (Then you answer your question based on their interests and what's important in their life.

2. Use positive directions against distress and addictions. I show clients how to do this in my consultation and coaching programs. The more you aim towards your positive directions, the sooner you'll be reaching your goals and dreams. Include aiming for being well-rested, well-nourished, well-exercised, and well-organized, and strive to always have something to look forward to.

What does this mean for you, and for all those you know? A lot. Your spirit needs you to play out your whole life as it was intended. Not like my student who cut hers short, without living fully, because of passing distress. You want to be remembered for all the positive things you've done, not the last stupid thing.

NOW, by starting with yourself, do you have ANY questions or objections to these rules for yourself?

If so, I am offering a Free Gift of a 20-minute personal session to answer any questions or concerns you have about this.

Simply sign in at https://calendly.com/drinafried

Choose one of the available times, mark your calendar. It will be confirmed. I'll meet you then.

Chapter 11
Three Crucial Teaching Times; Confusing Hurting Yourself

You might confuse nuances of what hurting yourself or another means.

Does going skydiving qualify as hurting yourself? No, not if you have carefully studied how to do it, have made sure that all safety features are in place, and just as importantly, you have also made sure that you are strong and healthy enough for that activity.

Regardless, if you are the one in a million when an accident still occurs, and you were to die, even though you have very carefully planned and stayed alert – well then- so be it! At least others feel normal grief from a bona fide accident, while you are doing something you regard as worthwhile to accomplish in your lifetime. Similarly, with being a respected professional such as a fireman, you might die saving others.

Generally, the kind of regrets and terrible concerns aren't there that are present when somebody commits suicide or acts of homicide. Suicide and homicide haunt the living differently, often generationally. They cause Post Traumatic Stress Disorders that rarely resolve or fade, causing some to resort to addictive or forever medications that promise to end symptoms, but very often have dangerous side effects, and also numb your good feelings.

Three Crucial Teaching Times:
Addressing Aggression Towards Another
and Towards Oneself

AGE	AGGRESSION	WITHIN SELF
1. Child on your lap	Slaps you (or another in your charge.)	Slaps self
2. Sometime during Grades 1-9	Bullies or plans to retaliate to get even	Is bullied or invites hurt (e.g., "Go ahead, punch me" "Hit me.")
3. Adulthood before any tragedy	Attracted to gang like thinking, terrorist, or involved in tactics of intimidation, plans for assassinations, and attacks to control.	Making harmful choices that lead to addictions, self-belittlement, suicidal planning and thoughts.

Chapter 12
Clear Out Past and Current Negative Emotions to Recover Rational Flexible Thinking and to Feel Relaxed and Loving

Choose at least one of these four ways to clear out your past distress, and to prevent new distress from piling on.

1. The Natural Way

When something goes wrong in your life, in a movie, in the news, in a story, book, etc. in my opinion it is very often because somebody has physically or psychologically hurt somebody or themselves. They don't have conscious rules not to hurt themselves or other people. Watch and listen as you go about living. See if you experience that, or not.

As I'm sure you know, negative emotions happen to you and others. (Fear, Anger, Grief, Boredom and in a different way,

Physical Pain and Tension.) Believe it or not, that's really all of the negative emotions there are, although Shakespeare would tell you differently. Negative emotions produce peptides/chemicals in your body, and then are either immediately released or are stored somewhere in your body.

Suspend your confusion or disbelief for about 5 minutes, maybe 6, if you will, because you will become an expert at helping your young people understand their own feelings if you allow me to explain:

Think of each emotion (feeling) as on a continuum. I'm going to tackle each emotion for you, so you can really understand the mild to severe nature of emotions:

Have you heard of peptides? Most haven't, but it originated in 1905 to describe any of a group of compounds consisting of two or more amino acids linked by chemical bonding between their respective carboxyl and amino groups. Peptides are what occurs in your body, when you feel emotions.

For example, think of **sadness/grief** as a gradient from:

Small disappointment ...all the way up to the worst grief and losses one can have. Call that a 10, the most possible. All the same type of sadness peptides/chemicals are being produced and stored in your body during sadness, just a smaller to a larger amount.

1 2 3 4 5 6 7 8 9 10

Got it?

Next think of **anger** on a continuum from:

Small irritations and little frustrations... ...all the way to the heaviest rage and disempowerment one can have. All the same anger peptides/chemicals are produced and stored in your body, just less amounts for the lighter feelings at 1,2,3---- ----and more for the heavier angry feelings-----8,9,10.

1 2 3 4 5 6 7 8 9 10

Also, can be thought of as light to heavy anger.

Are you getting it? Does this way of thinking about feelings make sense to you?

Next think of **fear** on this continuum from:

slight embarrassment to very embarrassed, all the way up to the worst anxiety, threat and terror one can have. All the same fear/anxiety peptides/chemicals are being produced, and then stored in your body.

1 2 3 4 5 6 7 8 9 10

Is this Nov. 2022 AARP Bulletin article, a rush to medicate rather than deal naturally with fears? You be your judge:

"Task Force Calls for Routine Anxiety Testing

"This is, I think, sorely needed and sorely overdue," says Robert Hudak, M.D., a psychiatrist at the University of Pittsburgh Medical Center Western Psychiatric Hospital.

Anxiety disorders are among the most common mental health issues in the United States, with more than 15 percent of adults reporting symptoms of anxiety in 2019, according to the Centers for Disease Control and Prevention. And that was before COVID-19.

Untreated anxiety can lead to clinical depression and can have an impact on everything from blood pressure to ulcers and chronic pain disorders....

One concern is that placing older people on some anti-anxiety drugs can cause side effects like impaired cognition and an increased risk of falls, the National Institutes of Health says.

Wouldn't you be interested in avoiding the bad side effects of antianxiety drugs on people younger than 64 as well? Also, I bet that antianxiety drugs only mask symptoms, and do not get rid of the fear itself, i.e., clear out the peptide/chemicals stored in the body following fearful experiences. Natural fear release, as described below, clears out the peptide/chemicals stored in the body. Furthermore, once one starts antianxiety drugs, wouldn't they be expected to remain on such pre-scribed drugs for as long as they lived; perhaps becoming dependent on them, otherwise going back to their original anxiety?

Now on to **Boredom** on the painful emotion continuum:

A little boring... up to hour after hour, day after day of massive boredom and restlessness, as sometimes was the case in school classrooms. All the same boring peptides/chemicals being produced and stored in your body.

1 2 3 4 5 6 7 8 9 10

There's an old bull fighter quote or saying, *"I'd rather be gored than bored."*

Lastly there's **physical pain and tension** on the continuum from:

Mild discomfort ... all the way to injuries with worse and worse physical tension and pain that one can have. All the same pain peptides/chemicals being produced and stored in your body.

1 2 3 4 5 6 7 8 9 10

Hard to believe, yet after the initial injury creates pain, making one need to scream and/or cry for a while. Then when the pain subsides, it's yawns, stretching and scratching that are the main manifestation of releasing old pain and tension. Let yourself experience this emotional release, one full yawn and stretch after another, and relieve any itching with scratching (scratching that's not overly aggressive). I found it energizing. What result will you have? Isolate yourself or be with others who understand, and will you please not heckle each other, so you won't feel the need to cover your mouth. (It's not possible to stretch and yawn fully if you cover your mouth. Right?)

Each of these 6 feelings in the body apparently secretes different peptide chemicals. When I was doing my dissertation on negative emotions and their release, in a science magazine article about how onion tears were compared with tears released when crying from grief, different peptides/chemicals were found in each of those two sets of tears. The crying tears were said to contain chemicals found to be in depressed people, but those peptides were NOT in tears released due to onion exposure. After I received the Ed.D. doctorate degree in the 1980's, I moved, and lost that article, so I can't give you that source.

Why is this important? Because storing up these emotional/ feeling peptides/chemicals in the body shuts down clear, flexible, creative and rational thinking, which in turn creates irrational decisions and unhelpful reactions. You have stored up all these negative emotions, mostly unconsciously, but now you are aware. All these past stored up peptides/and chemicals prevent your acumen, high intelligence, prowess, i.e. your genius potential. Is this a surprise to you? Most people haven't been taught this before.

So, when you talk to young people, as I practiced with my son- beginning when he was a toddler- It was effective to tell him what I observed by his facial expressions and body language. I simply made statements! No more is needed! No analysis. I just listened, observed, and stated it. "You look a little angry"….. "You seem to be sad" Done! You can do it too. You'll be teaching them not to be afraid of feelings. You will instead be helping them become more aware of their emotions. Another important result is that they will grow up being able to distinguish how emotions differ from thoughts.

For example, *"You are angry, huh?" "It's frustrating, right?" "You look scared. You're safe here though."* That's what I reported to my son when we were riding on a bouncy tractor-cart when I took him to a farm to pick our own fruit. He visibly relaxed when I simply said, *"You feel scared, and you think something bad will happen. But we are safe."* And we were, thank goodness. When you tell young people how they seem to feel, in this reporting manner, they will relax and think you have understood them. If you are mistaken in their feeling(s) as you are reporting to them, as their language increases, they will tell you that you are wrong. "No", I'm feeling more (e.g. embarrassed, or whatever they do feel.) You have taught them to be aware of their emotions, and also how emotions differ from thoughts. To what end? Because this is an important lesson for people, and it is a bonding moment between you and them, increasing their respect for you.

In order to stop negative emotions from taking hold of you in the first place, change what thoughts you say to yourself about them, right away. (Supplant your most likely negative thought with a positive direction, as a first line of defense.) Think it, not aloud is best, as it is usually a negative thought that you should not be reciting to yourself. <u>Turn it around and force yourself to create a positive sentence</u>. This is where your natural release of emotions, that you were born with, but learned to suppress as you grew up, comes into play.

This is actually a very good thing ----if (and it's a big IF) society" didn't do everything it could do (even "pacifiers") to stop the noise of the child when you were an infant and toddler rather than encouragement to let it out until it was ALL GONE, and you were relaxed and happy again. Yes, give the child what is necessary as quickly as you see it, or know it. (Such as food, water, warm or cooler clothing, a diaper change, cuddling, attention.) Giving this nurturing will stop their need for it, so it won't take long. That prevents negative emotions from building up in the first place.

Adults rarely if ever were given this type of nurturing and permission to discharge while they were children. Were you given freedom to discharge and release your emotions freely as a child growing up? So now, when you try to release through crying, profuse laughing and screaming, etc. as a grown adult, it feels awkward because society didn't do everything it could do (and instead now offers a valium, a cigarette, a few drinks, etc.) rather than encouragement to let out the old emotions. Now new emotional events can happen, and it would be preferable to release as soon as possible after the emotional event, until it was finished releasing, and was all gone. It's just "discharging" or releasing emotions on the spot.

Thus, you've created a sentence or two (which hopefully you have written down, or too often will quickly be forgotten) that will help you laugh, cry, shudder, or one of the other discharges of emotions mentioned below. Write down your positive message to yourself. You may find it valuable (as I did and do) by saying 180° the opposite thought, because then it can start the emotional release. (It could be through laughing, talking, crying with sobbing, tantruming [which is violent arm and fist movements in the air, or stamping, etc.] yawning, perspiration, active kidneys, and shivering/shaking.) Don't worry, not all at once! AND only depending on which emotions (are coming off of you at that time. After you release them all, through your discharge, you will be uplifted as you go on with your day(s).

You can't be bored while you are actually speaking. You as a teacher can help students keep out of boredom by using this information to get them to quickly talk to each other. My favorite is how all the students get to talk with each other in a period of a minute, maybe two minutes: You can integrate it with schooling by stopping after you've taught a lesson or several points. (They've been taught prior how to quickly pair up, when teacher grabs her stopwatch, kept nearby.)

You as teacher say: "Pair up and quickly decide who goes first" (as the speaker)"; the other person automatically becomes the listener. The students have been prior instructed when this technique was introduced to give warm aware good attention to their partner, even if their partner is silent, only thinking. My drill was *"You have (30) seconds* (Sometimes one minute, -whatever time that gets the interaction quickly completed, and the students rapidly back again, ready for what's next). *"You have 30 seconds* to say all you can remember about (name the title of your lesson.) "Go!" (time it)…. "Time up, Switch … Go." These interactions are best tight, full of student interaction, then back to the job of listening to the teacher's lesson, directions, etc. Afterwards, you might say something you thought is important to remember about the lesson, or ask: "Anybody have anything to share about what they learned?" (Silence?) Move on.

Heavy fear discharges through shuddering, cold skin and "eeeeek" type yells. Heavy anger releases through warm sweating, quick arm movements, and "nnnnnn", or "rrrrrrr" growling sounds. Unfortunately, we have learned to hate and worry about these sounds maybe leading to violence, so would rather people shut up. This heavy release is mostly at the upper numbers 8-10 on the continuum.

Let me tell you about the time I hurt my back while packing and moving to another house. My physician wanted to admit me to the hospital. By then I'd read everything I could about natural emotional release. I knew that if I was just allowed to scream while the pain was there, it would most quickly dissi-pate. I declined to be hospitalized, screamed and cried inter-mittently for about 1.5 days at home, and I was totally better. I asked people around me to either cover their ears, or I went into the bathroom and screamed into the toilet- so neighbors wouldn't hear me and think I was being murdered.

One more crucial point about feelings. Think of some of these emotions as being MIXED TOGETHER. That means you would use two or even three of the discharge methods at once, to get rid of that negative emotion, and to think about where the feelings originated during past happenings. Re-mind yourself, "*I felt afraid long ago. I am safe and wiser now.*"

For example, depression seems to be anger AND sadness mixed together. (And sure enough, when I and others that I coach went through some situational depression, it dis-charged rather quickly using the releases of crying with sob-bing - combined with an amount of righteous storming warm perspiration and angry sounds.) Writing out a direction to repeat over and over, such as "*What's the best thing to do next! What have I learned from this?*" *What can I do to avoid this in the future?*" Repeat this all the while discharging and noticing what other helpful thoughts come up. Write those down. Keep a notebook of your positive directions, to have on hand in your wallet or handbag, car, or nightstand; to remind you.

Jealousy? Jealousy seems to be a mixture of fear, anger, dis-appointment, and often some embarrassment. These feelings discharge too, using the aforementioned physiological releases of fear, anger, and sadness. I use a chart when coaching people as to how to discharge/release safely. You compare the feeling (looking all quiet on the outside but feeling bad inside you). The release of the feeling is later when you have gotten yourself in a safe place; otherwise, you are likely to be misunderstood and thought unusual by some others who don't understand the discharge process. The release of feelings versus the internal feeling is quite different. Then *write down the opposite of your thinking*. This stops the rehearsing of those "poor me", negative thoughts, and soon one is laughing, shuddering, reluctantly or animatedly talking (to another listener who understands the emotional release process and isn't interested in prolonging your jealously). Tell God, talk to the steering wheel, wherever you are safe from being mocked for discharging. For example, *"I was lucky to get rid of him/her now, before I invested even more into the relationship."* Jealousy has caused much trouble for people who don't have a rule against harming others, as their thoughts and actions are wasted on planning revenge. What a shame. So here too, never stop trying. "Infinite hope, endless endeavor."

Surely you understand that there is not and was never a lot of money to be made using this natural method. Pharmaceutical companies would rather you buy their medications. I recently read what to me are shocking numbers of hundreds of thousands of people being on antidepressants- for over five years; and are fearful of stopping and "going back to square one". I (and you too?) look at it that the depressed peptide/chemicals remain in place in their brain and cells, thus hindering their healing by keeping those peptides in place in the body. Add that many people, while we learned to reclaim our ability to release the negative emotions were embarrassed and scared (see fearful) of doing it at first; because as you grew older you learned to hold it in- due to- yes fear- fear of being ridiculed. Once you relearn how <u>not</u> to hold it in, all the releases become as fun as a laugh fest. Laughing feels good, and so does crying with sobbing, and even shaking with your body shuddering, UNLESS you're rehearsing/repeating/rethinking negative THOUGHTS while crying and shuddering. If you concoct proper positive directions, it feels good to release it over time. This is where I'd like to say, "Trust me and try it".

So, learning to think of the complete opposite thoughts saves the day. Let me tell you about when I was trying to get myself to exercise back in 1979. (I couldn't jog even for 5 minutes at first. I read Covert Bailey's *"Fit or Fat"*, which essentially said to keep jogging <u>without stopping</u> - no matter how slowly - at about 80% of your capacity. 12 minutes will suffice.) My opposite self-talk became, *"I'm the fastest runner in the world!"* Lots of chuckling with that, although for the first time ever I was going in the right direction, as I lied to myself - and knew it of course. *I'm the fastest runner in the world, indeed*! However, I kept it up and jogged for 350 or more days per year, building up to a half hour to 45 minutes each day from 1980-2016. Then I fell in the streets of NYC on my way to do an art show in Barcelona. I ended up with a cane there, and then a physician convinced me my 36 years of jogging were now over. Before the fall, I had actually hoped to BE the fastest 100-year-old female jogger ever.

Back in the 1970's about 30ish% of the population of Santa Barbara, CA used this natural discharge method, many adding the positive direction verbiage. People would hold each other's hands while they took their turn discharging (releasing the old chemicals), and one would be the designated listener and the other the emotional releaser; dividing whatever time they had in half for each person's "turn". I went to co-counseling classes led by Beth Streuver in Rochester, NY, went to England and all over the United States, especially while Mary McCabe was with Harvey Jackins's leadership. Then I coached and taught others in central California.

If it's too late, and you were told to STOP (stop crying, be quiet- don't talk [either reluctantly or animatedly], stop yawning, stop shaking, stop screaming) you'll maybe notice how so many negative emotion peptides/chemicals got stored in your body from years ago, often from as early as before you could talk.

Past negative feelings became buried inside you from when you were young. Not releasing these negative emotions that got into you became chronic because you were discouraged from using the natural physiological method, as you were born being able to do.

From now on, better to allow yourself to change that. Stop using postures and techniques that HOLD-IN emotional release at least where it's safe to do so. To reiterate, sorry, when the negative emotions drain off you, you'll be left with the ability to act in a relaxed, rational, flexible, creative, and appropriate manner. You won't be influenced by negative thoughts as much, or at all, which otherwise contribute to more fear, frustration, anger, sadness, tension, boredom, and even pain.

My favorite self-example of releasing fear is when I was in my early 30's. I was too embarrassed to sing in front of people. So, I didn't. I had a good singing voice back then, really did, said my choir teacher in High School. I figured out that my choking up was all related to fear chemicals. I estimated I had 40ish hours of bottled-up fear chemicals in me. It took a while to discharge that stored up fear; hours of shaking away old fear, while reminding myself "I can sing beautifully wherever I go, in front of whomever I want. My triumph of conquering that terror was in Chicago at the time of the release of the first "Star Wars". I was at the American Psychological Association and Albert Ellis, a prominent psychologist at the time, asked me to come up in front of about 2000 people and sing one of the songs he wrote. I did, and got somewhat of a standing ovation, even though no one else there knew that public singing used to terrorize me. Since then, I was asked to speak on a couple of cruise ships (2 tickets in the Mediterranean area for 2 weeks was lovely), and I added in stress management songs to which I wrote lyrics, accompanying myself with a forgiving Omnichord, while giving my stress management talks in those days. I was asked to sing "the Star-Spangled Banner" at a Mohammed Ali event, but I must have been a second choice because I wasn't given advanced notice on my answering machine until that afternoon, and I didn't see it until too late.

What does this mean for you? Quite a bit. What could YOU accomplish in your day-to-day life, to be prouder and happier with yourself (while also humble) if you started releasing some of your old negative fears and sadness, etc. that got stored inside you? It would simply be old hurt coming off, leaving you relaxed and fearless, able to accomplish more and more easily. As my partner says, *"Circumstances don't cause the quality of our life. Our thoughts determine how we feel. Our feelings determine what we do; and what we do creates our results."* So, by letting yourself discharge your negative emotions you are left feeling relaxed, content, and zestful. Your thoughts will in turn become more rational and those thoughts will be your best guide to action.

See the Bibliography to get *"The Human Side of Human Beings"* if you're interested in finding out how it all got started. One of my clients was miffed with me for only suggesting this tiny inexpensive book, but for not insisting that he read it right away. Much was revealed to him by reading it. All this above is the author's interpretation of the theory of emotions in humans versus inanimate objects, presented in *The Human Side of Human Beings*. Of course, it is your choice, although I suggest you find and read it too. Rational Island Press http://www.rc.org literary section. This group is progressive.

Ask the adult(s) you know, *"What are you going to be left with if you consciously take a rule not to hurt yourself?* Note what THEY say… I say that your life will get better and better. And when you are under stress, you won't harm yourself or others too. You'll be clear about finding other ways of solving difficult situations -flexibly and creatively. That will leave you happier, and grateful for what you have accomplished.

Ask yourself, over time, what YOU feel and think for having these 2 rules, and for practicing offensiveless defense.

If you give this method a try, and **don't** want to use it, here are three other methods to reduce negative emotions which have been developed in present time. I'm not speaking about prescribed or over the counter drugs or supplements. Prescribed medication is between you and your physician.

2. Your Electric Body Cataloged with Thousands of Blueprint Frequencies

Every nerve pulse in your body is an electrical current traveling. Every cell in your body is basically a mini-pump, a mini-battery that is pumping about 70 to 90 millivolts when you are healthy. Below 70, disease starts to take place. You don't do well. You are more prone to disease and illnesses, not having energy levels up to where they need to be. That is important. In fact, every muscle in your body is powered by a chemical reaction. The food that you eat is like the fuel that you'd put into your car, or into a generator to generate electricity. The quality of that fuel, in this case the food, determines how well your little mini-pumps work. How much clean healthy energy they can produce. Not just the food, but even the way you think! The better you think, the better you eat, the better you drink to stay dehydrated, is going to determine how well those mini-battery pumps work in your body. When there is no more energy left in the cell, that's when everything stops. In fact, death is termed the absence of energy.

The invention is a tool or module you can have, or have scanned on you, or by you if you were to own one of these current scanners. The scanner I decided to invest in even has 204 food sensitivity items that are able to be looked at and scanned. These are things you might have that you are allergic to or have an adverse reaction to, that your body is not capable of processing at this point. One example of the 1204 list of items is dairy (such as butter, cottage cheese, cheddar cheese, goats' milk, goats' cheese, processed cheese, etc. Your score is from 1 to 9 and if you score 1 or 9, you would be better off avoiding those foods. They say that can change over time. Of their 204 items the frequency scanner also checks for most meats, various nuts, fruits, gluten, yeast, other grains, various beans, legumes, seafoods, seeds, spices, eggs, etc. If you are shown to be sensitive, it is best to avoid those foods and just eat within the middle range. Outside of the middle range is too much work for the body to break that down. Just avoid the items that will cause an issue and focus on the items that cause you no issue. Better fuel, better energy. The more work your body must do to breakdown the food, the less energy your cells are going to have. So many of the problems you have can be related to your gut. Food you are not processing or digesting right, you're not drawing out the nutrients that are in the food. It may not go well with the acidic level in your stomach. It could activate other enzymatic reactions.

The Inner Voice Scan identifies unconscious emotions and sends you a program to simply listen to daily (also through headphones) which is said to affect your emotional peace of mind and create optimal wellbeing.

As another example, using frequency signatures, chakras, you can scan and get at that moment in time, the emotion as well as the flower. For example, the CEO did his scan, and it came up with "despair and crab apple", the flower. It might not seem to make sense, because he said he did not feel any despair, but added "Maybe deep inside there's some issue going on." So, they solved it by imprinting some sugar pellets, or a ring, or semi-precious stone bracelet with homeopathic version frequencies of many diseases (e.g. T.B.) much like a vaccine works; like kills like. Which is an oversimplification of how homeopathic works. Guessing and muscle testing become not necessary.

Your homeopathic remedy is made right then and there, without having to go out and buy that remedy, or buy anything else. Let's say you had acne scars, so you would click on that symptom from over 3600 symptoms. The scan comes up with the homeopathic remedies that are most commonly used for that particular condition, and imprints it into your item, that you then wear, or suck on, in the case of sugar pellets.

The instrument is called Solex AO Scan Technology. Their CEO is Loran Swensen. They asked questions and found frequency solutions. There are other new instruments that may resemble this technology, but I decided to study and use the Solex. [https://youtu.be/CJjli9m4bAO https://shop.solexnation.com/artbydrina/Application?type=3]

"This is an elegant yet simply designed technology inspired by discoveries from Tesla, Einstein, and many other renowned scientists. It is designed to communicate with the body via subtle bio-frequencies and electromagnetic signals.

3. A Rife Frequency Machine

Software that you play through earphones for a set time after you set frequencies to play which have been programmed to mitigate symptoms that you have chosen to be targeted.

I am currently trying out Life Frequencies Pro X8 software. I found Brian Zeleniak at a Naturopathic convention in Las Vegas in Oct. 2022. http://www.bztronics.com email: info@bztronics.com Life Frequencies does not use multi-level marketing. The Rife Life Frequencies was a one-time invest-ment for just under $500, more affordable than AO scan.

Currently the AO scan investment is about the price of the Rife frequency software. For that you get their hardware, which is a handheld device that also contains a phone, etc. THEN you have a monthly Solex fee for running their vari-ous programs. Solex encourages you to join their multilevel marketing program to get them clients, and you get compen-sated to pay your monthly upgraded software (which you can turn off,) and also to earn part-time or full-time income if you wish. I have chosen not to engage in earning so far. However, fair warning, if and when I have online, virtual, and/or in-person seminars, consultations and coaching pro-grams, I may offer to do AO scanning of the Inner Voice, SEFI, and Rapid and Comprehensive Body Scans.

These two advanced systems are similar in that they both use frequencies and are continually updated at this point. They are also quite different. A difference is that you choose which Rife symptoms to target, from your conscious mind. The AO scan scans you and tells you what symptoms and sensitivities are showing up at that time. Many scan themselves daily or weekly. Then you can choose those frequencies (or others for that matter) to run, use, and/or program to listen to, to make homeopathic pellets or program frequencies into rings, brace-lets, etc., and even what color glasses to wear, with what flower to resonate, and what foods or items to avoid due to sensitivities.

4. A Psychosomatic Approach to Healing & Freeing Your Thoughts, Emotions, & Behaviors - Heal the Pattern Once and for All

Zero Point is a powerful online intensive led by Gabriel Cousens, M.D., M.D.(H), D.D., a family therapist and acknowledged spiritual teacher. Dr. Cousens teaches a series of techniques that identify and release inhibiting mental, emotional and behavioral patterns. These techniques are particularly applicable to limiting or damaging core beliefs and addictions.

Dr. Cousens' approach works to get directly to the energetic origin of an issue, rather than treating on the surface level of intellectual understanding or awareness without truly dissolving the blockage.

Dr. Cousens teaches that our essential nature is inherently free in all ways. What obscures this freedom is the fact that most of us live in a self-induced trance, identified with the stories of our past, future, and present. In the evolution of consciousness, the realization of one's deepest nature of freedom is just the beginning of the awakening process.

Dr. Cousens teaches that our personality (ego) is a case of mistaken identity. In self-realization, we do not dissolve the ego, but learn to use it as a tool in the world. To feel true inner peace, freedom, joy, and love, we must confront and transmute our out-moded patterns of operation that obstruct and inhibit the path to liberation.

"The goal of Zero Point is to teach us how to thrive spiritually, living from the vibrantly alive and free core of our unique souls. Zero Point helps participants to connect with their individual divine blueprint, to live empowered and to embrace life without fear, hesitation, or resistance."

https://www.drcousens.com/zeropoint
email: info@TreeOfLife.nu

Does all or any of this emotional/psychological and physical stuff work? Many say yes. I wouldn't be surprised if others will say no. Some will say it's nature, it's inherited. Regardless, it's worth trying to see if you succeed in ridding yourself of impairing negative emotions.

Get good second opinions from those without an agenda. Investigate yourself if that is you. The essentially free method is the first method above. Notable is that Tai Chi, Qi Gong, breathing exercises, yoga, meditation, martial arts, hypnosis and self-hypnosis, and similar are beneficial. However, they are not <u>directly</u> targeting getting rid of past and present negative emotions, as are the above four methods in this chapter.

Chapter 13
Recipe for Teaching Toddlers - Kindergarten the Two Rules – Easiest to Do

Toddlers really do want to cooperate and will do as you suggest, if they understand what you suggest, and as long as you haven't added much distress to them- by hurting them.

Child on your lap- even though their force is probably not harmful, (to you or to their siblings), still take this first opportunity to teach the child NOT to hurt another or themself:

Slaps you as hard as they can. Do not laugh, don't strike back, etc. Gently take their offending hand firmly, say *"NO!"* Put a nearby pillow (or similar soft item) in front of them, and lovingly SAY- *"Be gentle with people. No hurting anybody. Hit here (the pillow) instead!"* This is the great teaching opportunity. (He or she will usually bash the pillow for a long or short period of time, while you keep happily looking on.) Sometimes/often they will then switch and slap themselves.

Slaps themselves as hard as they (probably) can. Do as above - Do not laugh; gently take their offending hand; firmly say "NO!" Grab a nearby pillow (or similar) and lovingly SAY- "*Be gentle to yourself too. Hit here instead.*" Demo hitting the pillow, and he or she will usually bash the pillow for a long or short period of time while you continue to warmly look on, throughout it all, with interest. (When they stop hitting the pillow, they'll get off your lap and do something else- 99.9% chance of doing nothing harmful.) Lesson learned.

Teaching this usually takes about 5-10 minutes. Like "a stitch in time, saves nine", this 5-minute lesson often lasts a life-time. Thus, it works out best and easiest if training begins during this earliest toddler/preschool age.

If you have added distress to them- by hurting them; if you have harmed them in ANY way, say, "*I am sorry that I hurt you and said and/or did _____ to you. You didn't deserve that, and I apologize! (If you really mean it) It won't happen again. I now have a rule against doing and saying that sort of thing, and if I ever forget again, you say 'Stop it', that hurts, you told me to tell you to stop!*"

Please get in touch with a good counselor if you seem unable to stop adding distress and hurting them. Do the same if you also have the same trouble stopping with the grades 1 though adults as well.

Chapter 14
Second Most Crucial Teaching Time – Recipe for Teaching these 2 Rules - during Grades 1 through Grades 9

Bullying and teasing tops the list of children's school troubles: 86% of 12–15-year-olds said it occurred at their schools, ranking higher than racism, pressures to try drugs, or to have sex. One in five reported having been bullied. Bullying was most often just overlooked. Talk to your children about bullying, even if they don't bring it up. Let them know that you think it shouldn't happen.

Do not dismiss bullying as a part of growing up. It causes distress, and as mentioned before, so does teasing. Both are rarely, if ever, pleasant for the receiver.

With the person bullying:

In a school or home setting, it includes physical aggression and verbal assault: Either you are told about it or notice the bullying yourself.

You, the parent or teacher: Do not yell. Firmly say *"NO."* Add, *"I'm not going to let you hurt each other.* Although bullying is often ignored at school, students often report being victims. There is bullying in classrooms, in halls, on the bus, in the playground- and even on their computers. (This includes unwanted physical contact, verbal assault, making obscene gestures or even facial expressions, as well as being intentionally excluded.) Victims are exposed repeatedly over time, to intentional injury or discomfort inflicted by one or more other people. Teachers rarely detected bullying; Teachers intervened in only 4% of all incidents (noted in 1999). However, teachers are now being made more aware of bullying by students and by their parents. Perhaps with new awareness, things have improved...It's a long way though from 4% to satisfactory improvement in intervention.

Each time you coach someone to take the two rules of no harm, and to use offensiveless defense, you are improving the situation! Perhaps start by saying, *"People are not for hurting or putting down!"* Then ask, *"What happened?"* (If both the bullier and the victim are present, listen to their responses and repeat each response to the other person ("He said _____"; without judging, by going back and forth (S/he said _____" until a solution is found- best found by them.)

If the bullier seems to enjoy intimidating and hurting another, ask: "Did anybody ever do that to you?" (e.g., "pants" you) Often it's yes. Then say, "I'm sorry that happened to you. (Even yell:) It should never have happened!" Best if you can make light contact with both aggressor and victim (on their wrist or hand) as it keeps human connection, shows caring, and helps to calm the situation, without you saying the useless and incendiary, "Calm down!"

Sometimes ask, *"Were you two EVER friends?"* If yes, ask *"What is something you liked about him/her?"* Take time- WAIT until they come up with something.... (Maybe they both liked sports, math, maybe they both were nice, ---listen for anything.)

When a victim triggers the person bullying, it's usually that the bullier wants the victim to be more likable to them, or somehow change. As the teacher or parent, say, *"It only makes the situation and the person you bully worse by treating them badly. And all you probably really wanted was to do is have them not irritate you." Can you please simply accept others for who they are, and not try to change them? (Wait for an answer) Because It'll be too much to expect them to change."*

Finally ask the bully to answer this: *"Are you willing to never again treat anyone, including yourself, with anything less than complete respect?"* Some bullies are very receptive and some need careful convincing evidence. If they finally say they are willing, get a pen and paper; write it out, or have them clearly write that sentence.

Then have them say it aloud: *"From this moment forward, I sincerely (or happily) promise to never again treat anyone, including myself, with anything less than complete respect. This will mean _____."* Have the person being victimized do the same, say it and write it, when they agree. Tony Robbins calls the act of writing it down "a positive anchor" which deepens the commitment. Otherwise also, it is likely to be forgotten if not written down.

Then you can get them ready to use offensiveless defensive responses for the future. There are thousands of offensiveless defense responses. It is generally a matter of responding from the heart truthfully in that situation, with the idea of doing no harm. *"Let's quit this nasty talk and behavior and get along from now on!"* You can do this. You can do this now. You can do this right here."

With the person being victimized:

The child tells you, or you see them getting teased or bullied. Neither baby them nor rush off to GET the offending one (perhaps yet). First kindly and calmly ask for the details *"Tell me what happened?"* Listen carefully to their answers and reflect the feelings you think you notice: Say, *"You look (sad, angry, scared, embarrassed* (whatever emotion they seem to show). They will correct you if you're wrong. *I'm so sorry that happened*. (Even yell:) *It should never have happened! It's not your fault. Unfortunately, a lot of people get bullied. It's wrong. It's often a sign of weakness on their part, and their desire to feel superior*." If the attacked person starts to cry, touch them lightly on the shoulder or comfort them in an appropriate way that you know helps. Tell them to "*Let all your disappointment/anger/fear/frustration out. You will feel better if you also keep thinking, "We'll fix this problem together!*"

When they become relaxed and attentive, then say, "*I have some ideas of what to say and how to stop the bullying and teasing for the future.... will you let me show you?*" Wait for yes. Then show the victim 3-6 offensiveless defense responses, while you role-play being him or her responding back to the bullier.

1. Try using a sarcastic tone of voice **for put-downs**; or use humor) "*Very funny!*" "*You noticed it too!*" "*I see you're not prepared to like me. Oh well! Come back when you are.*" Suggest they try to smile and say, "*Are you saying you would you like me more if I _____, _____, or _____?*)

2. Defend yourself **using facts** (e.g., "*You don't have to tell me I'm (e.g., overweight), Thanks for caring though.*" I've got a mirror!*" So what!*", I bet I could beat you in chess". "*My mother dresses me funny to you, but she loves me.*"

3. Sometimes **use justification** (e.g., "*I like [doing] it like that!*"). "*I'm creating my own style!*"

Practice having them look you in (one of your) eyes while practicing the responses they seem to like the best (e.g., if they laugh at one of your offensiveless defense responses, that's a good response to write down to practice it for the future.)

Have them learn to express this idea: *"You could hurt me; I might hurt you too ; but it's really not good for us. We'd be better off helping each other, rather than trying to wreck each other."* Or say, *"Hurting me or you is not in anybody's best interest, and can lead to even more troubles, more problems. If you frighten me, I won't like you, and I WANT to like you! STOP bullying me so I can like you...."* (Most bullying is not well thought out.)

Write the words out clearly for them to practice, so they'll be ready for the future. (That's what the written word is for, to remember the directions in which for you to go.) Take all the time needed until they are ready. Ball up a coat or jacket, ready to have them repeatedly hit it, if you see anger. (To be sure, ask, *"Does _____ make you feel angry?"* If it's a different feeling, they will let you know.

Remind this age group that, *"Everything else, except hurting yourself or the other person, is okay to do. However, some ideas are better than others. (For example, although it's not a rule here not to take things that don't belong to you, it works out much better if you don't. People will respect you more, people who love you will trust you. Therefore, it's better if you ask to borrow what you want, ask to share, or ask how you can earn it.) The same with saying things that aren't true. Things work out better when you stick with the truth, even though it's not one of these two rules."*

When I've coached families, if you were to take somebody by the wrist and if you were to slowly dig in, you intuitively know the point where it goes into pain. You'll know if you pay attention. The same thing with verbal put-downs, and psychological slanders. By helping young people, as well as learning yourself, how not to cross those boundaries, you'll become stronger by defending yourselves without harming back the offending person. Do I need to mention that the "offending person" starts to realize that harming others doesn't get them what they think they want? However, the older they get, the slower the realization often can be.

Make yourself clear to this age group that still aren't adults. It might be some form of:

"When you _____ (explain by saying the exact details -so they know the irking part) *I get so angry that I want to bash you. I won't though because I don't want you to be hurt, I don't want you to dislike me, and I don't want you to stop being cooperative"*. Displacing such as this performs several functions:

   a. helps to get rid of your own irritation.

   b. it models offensiveless defense.

c. it distracts the young person from their misbehavior.

d. it gives you time to think of another proactive or redirected response. *"Our walls are not for writing. Write on this paper instead." "People are not for hitting, hit here (e.g., on this pillow) instead! Yes, do it until your anger is gone. I will be writing down some opposite thoughts of what's bothering you.*

By writing the opposite, and then having them repeat after you, saying the opposite, they will often start laughing, which will release a bunch of their frustration and anger. Also, by saying an opposite, it stops rehearsing the anger, repetition which would otherwise just make negative thoughts stronger. Saying the opposite more often than not, turns into the direction one really wants to go, and often will strike them as funny.

It's hard to believe this until you see it in action. Such fun to open up new ways to think positively. I hope you'll come to my online guidebook course and demonstrations. There you can see the magic that happens when a person repeats the opposite of their negative thoughts that have produced negative feelings. You see the change of these emotional releases. Fears are released too, and are dissipated, and clearer thinking happens. Do you understand that feelings will determine what you do, and this is not the best guide to action. Rational and clear thinking is what you want to determine what you do, thus creating your best result. The more you release the old negative emotions, the more you are left with the ability to think rationally and clearly.

This seems strange at first. Being uncomfortable with the natural release of fear (Fear of releasing fear) is perhaps what leads many people instead turn to medication to feel better, rather than taking a chance on knowing themselves more, usually releasing some old or current embarrassment, and then really feeling better when that's gone.

I hope you will bravely see what I mean someday. It doesn't hurt, this shaking, shuddering, and making noise, and it actually feels like good fun to safely release these negative emotions. No rush. In the meantime,

"Just say NO" to hurting yourself or anybody else, even so-called slightly. There are so many things that don't break those 2 rules. Know the difference and daily make those better choices for yourself.

Joy Hibbins in _Suicide Prevention Techniques- How A Suicide Crisis Service Saves Lives_, notes (pp.74-76) It's "not uncommon for a client to express extreme emotional pain through anger. However, anger can provoke strong feelings in the professional supporting them"....(in this case YOU supporting them).... "particularly likely to happen if the client is using swear words...." Ms. Hibbins explains that it's expressing "profound distress and pain and often emphasizes the loss of control that the person is experiencing at the time.... This may lead to the clinician warning the person that if they continue to use this kind of language, they will terminate the appointment or phone call...This can inflame the situation, increasing the person's sense of injustice and anger.... indeed fear, because the person"....was seeking help when they felt unable to live without significant assistance."

She rightly distinguishes between " 'descriptive swearing'... (This situation is ******* unbearable. I cannot ******* stand it anymore." Yet some clinicians were interpreting it as directed against them and responded with *"Don't swear at me"*. If they had been directing swearing at the clinician it would sound more like, "You are a *******" and categorized as verbal abuse then. She emphasizes the importance of focusing on "helping the person....allow the person to ventilate their anger to enable them to return to a calmer state....validate their emotion....understand why the person has experienced such intense rage....let the person express their anger at this point rather than....expecting them to suppress it....focus should be on them, rather than on how their anger....makes us (you) feel....We need to react in a supportive way to their anger."

You as a parent, teacher, grandparent, counselor, spouse, friend, lover, partner, student, sibling, aunt, uncle, cousin, coworker, can tackle this by reporting their feelings back to them, "You're really angry about (repeat some of the situation they have said, back to them). and asking if they are willing to take each of the two rules, and listening to their response, even if objections. Ms. Hibbins describes situations (pp.132-135) when young people and adults are perceived as a person "who cannot be helped" ....it is only a matter of time before he or she will end their life. When this stage is reached, it is likely that "the person has simply not found the right kind of help yet.... Assume that a change of approach or even a change of service may be indicated....the responsibility we bear in trying to provide a service which is tailored to the individual and which meets their needs....to help a person to engage....How do we ensure that we provide what they need, or if we feel we can't, then how do we help them to access a service which can?." Or "if a person is engaging but appears not to be improving.... particularly when someone is self-harming or attempting suicide frequently that clinicians start to talk in terms of the inevitability of death" Hibbins believes and I concur, "they should be under an obligation to explore all other avenues outside their own local....referring...for an independent assessment...in another part of the country...."

However, for your purposes with your young people and students, and adults who concern you, "persistently retain the belief that" (yours) "can survive.... we need to be tenacious in helping them....to work persistently to provide or find the help that they need. We should never stop trying. Infinite hope, endless endeavor."

Chapter 15
Last Chance - Recipe for Teaching these 2 Rules to Adults

When working with adults, it's more like asking for acceptance rather than teaching. Gently introduce these ideas, because the person is no longer being raised by parents or under school authority.

Sometimes I've introduced the subject by telling people in their late teens, 20's, 30's, and 40's about a study I heard about: This study involved asking subjects, the eldest of the oldest people they could find: "If you could go back to ANY age, to what age would YOU choose?"

To my coaching clients, I'd say "You aren't very old yet, so what age do you think most of these old people chose for themselves? I'd wait. I waited until they came up with their answer, before telling the results of the study. It pretty much doesn't matter what my young adults answered. What matters is the study's results: The majority of elders answered that they would go back to the decade of their 50's! I would've thought most would choose younger. But no. Most chose going back to ages 50-59.

What is so valuable about this study? People in their late teens to early 20's are most likely to commit acts of assault. You want them to conclude that the best in their lives is yet to come. You want them to know that there is a bright future ahead, as long as they don't mess it up by harming themselves and/or others. Explain that by taking these two rules and using offensiveless defense, they would have the best chance of going on to a greater future. You want them to know that the best results will happen if they don't ruin it by harming themselves and/or others physically and psychologically in the meantime.

Please feel free to tell your people about this study, and what makes it so important for them.

It's not likely that I'll get to meet your people. This is what I talk to groups about. If there is a group you'd like me to speak with, my personal assistant's number is (702)283-1795.

Why do women need to care about concussions?

In an August 2022 article in *Prevention Magazine* about "The Brain Injury Overlooked In Women" Megan Rabbit explains how concussions cause a range of symptoms even more dangerous in women than in men. Anatomical differences such as women tending to have smaller and weaker necks makes them more vulnerable to the rotation of forces that can injure the brain. We hear more about discussions of concussions involved in males playing sports such as football.

Most shocking to this author, your Drina, is the statement that "one in three women falls victim to intimate partner violence at some point in her life." This is according to the Brain Injury Association Of America, and they add, "a victim of intimate partner abuse will often be hit in the head area. "We've had countless victims tell us that their abuser hit them on the head because their hair would hide their bruises," says Dr. Zieman, M.D., a neurologist at the Concussion And Brain Injury Center at Barrow neurological institute.

Dr. Zieman runs one of the few programs focused on treating traumatic brain injury and survivors of domestic violence. In a 2017 retrospective study by this Institute, it was noted that traumatic brain injury is a frequent consequence of domestic violence. "Our main finding was the sheer number of injuries and also the frequency. Victims are hit in the head many times over many years – so many times they've lost count and their symptoms persist and are often quite severe." 81% of subjects reported they had lost consciousness at least once and yet the victims often don't seek treatment. The article suggests that anyone who has been assaulted to their head should go to check if it is a concussion and seek treatment if it is. Even when they do if they are there, for example, for a broken arm, the ER doctor may not bring up brain injury. The most profound thing that these women endure is cognitive problems particularly relating to memory, attention, organization, and planning that often prevent them from holding down a job or performing everyday tasks. It also "makes it harder for them to plan a way to leave their abuser."

I hope you see too where I'm going with this, so that you can go there too: that you will use this knowledge to make sure that not only you know now -but also you will bring it up to your young people -males and females- preferably even before they start to date.

Make it known that this has to stop. Love is not enough for a relationship. There must be boundaries! In my opinion an extremely important boundary is that there be no violence, no harming of each other, in a relationship.

My life was changed when I decided to take and adhere to these two rules of no harming. This is when I came up with the concept of offensiveless defense. I don't want you to "turn the other cheek". You need a way to stop these unwanted subtle and not-so subtle attacks. Sometimes with a kind voice, sometimes with a strong statement, always without meanness and bullying back. It took a while before I really knew the importance of offensiveless defense. From then on, I had mostly "Blessed Days".

(Sure, I've had accidents which ruined things for a while- you live long enough- you will too most likely- like when I fell and crushed my left hip, 15 days in hospital, titanium rod, then Deep Vein Thrombosis and 2 more hospital days. I used to fall once or twice yearly when I jogged from 1980-2016. But then I could get right up and go treat the external wound.) Anyway, my point here is that I made sure that anybody I would plan on getting close to also had these two rules. You would probably be making a mistake if you stayed in any relationship if the rule of not harming another person is broken, maybe even the first time. It's your choice whether to give a second chance. Maybe if you and other people put these rules up on the wall at home, your guests would know to follow them. Especially if you lead by example. However too often severe abusers (without these rules) repeat offenses. It's impossible to avoid frustration and anger in life completely. However, remember to bash your pillow, not the person.

To adults who are putting themselves down, or are self-abusive in any way, they are also more susceptible to suicide: Say, "It seems like you haven't yet taken a rule NOT to hurt yourself (physically and psychologically)." (Listen to their response) Address what they say, yet mostly listen.

Next ask, "In view of all that you've said, has anybody ever specifically <u>asked</u> you to take a rule to never (again) hurt yourself?"

(Listen carefully again, in order to address any objections to taking the rule, if any come up. For a self-hating egocentric individual, you may need to ask, "Do you think it would be good for ME to hurt myself?" (Listen for them to say No.) "Well, YOU are a person too."

Finally ask: a) "Are you willing to take a rule from this day forward not to hurt yourself?" When you get a "yes", add: "Good, and it's important that you always keep and hold that rule, and watch where your life goes. Nobody has ever lived forever, so you'll get to experience your passing away. Live fully until your time comes. That's what humans were meant to do; not to rush it up;"

Chapter 16
What If You Are Wanting to Rehabilitate an Adult Headed Towards Criminal Incarceration, Unless They Were to Change Their Ways?

Rehabilitation of an adult already in the criminal justice system -or-stopping one who is likely headed that way, later or now, is a most difficult intervention.

The Stance You Take Especially When Dealing With Difficult People:

a)   As a parent or a teacher working with difficult young people, you will often need to put on a (figurative) mask. This mask is to stop yourself from letting frustration and anger into YOU- due to the adult or student's current or ongoing pattern of negative behavior.

b) When you speak, only use a "Please pass the salt" tone of voice. I hope you know what I mean- it's a calmer way of speaking. You can practically say almost anything to almost anybody, just by using a *"Please pass the salt"* tone of voice. What to say if it's not self-evident? Perhaps ask for clarification: *"It looks like you guys* _____ (aren't getting along. What's happening?)" *"It seems like* _____ (something's going on that could bring on some trouble?)"

Practice modulating your voice to use that tone when you can't stop yourself from criticizing- whoops- giving advice, to a young person or adult. See if they take it more in stride rather than getting a hurt, angry, or a disgusted look on their face. If you're especially wise about your interaction or suggestion, perhaps they'll surprise you with cooperation.

c) Listen and let them verbally argue if they wish, to know their thinking, and to let them vent a bit. (Talking is another wonderful emotional release, as it actually gets rid of frustration, embarrassment, and even boredom beautifully- especially if you can let them talk long enough, although rarely does anybody let somebody talk long enough while being listened to well). Also, by listening and allowing them to verbally argue with you, it will help you later address any of their irrational thoughts with reason. (See step d). Do not take on their arguing tone of voice! Just put on your warm, aware, relaxed, and **interested** facial expression as you gaze into (one of) their eyes. Be the adult who gives good attention.

d) Stay aware that your relaxed stance will keep alive the natural affection between you as the helper, and them - the authentic adult underneath that bullier exterior, which developed sometime earlier in their lifetime. Maybe they caught it like one catches a common cold, by mostly being around others who bully.

e) Tell them, *"I understand that you (used to)* **think** (repeat a thought or two of theirs from step c) so they realize you are a good listener, *"and it made you* **feel** *unhappy and frustrated, even angry.*

f) Remind them to keep their agreement not to harm others, if they had previously heard it. If, to your knowledge they haven't yet taken the rule not to harm others, suggest taking the rule not to harm others, as in the last Chapter; *"Regardless, people are not for hurting. They are for getting along with, for uplifting, and at worst, just let them be."* (Do you dare say "Laissez faire"?

By you doing this work with those you know, you will likely stop their being bullied, suicide ideation, assaults and battery, and the harm in between those extremes. Consequently, you will be responsible for much less emotional pain (less need to grieve, be sad, worried, embarrassed, frustrated, fearful, and angry), even if you'll never know for sure that it was due to YOUR influence. You and they will be able to think more clearly too. Why? Because negative emotions cause people to shut down, thus becoming confused and ineffective. By helping people, including yourself, to release and get rid of past negative emotions, you will be more relaxed, rational, content, and even zestful.

When a situation is brewing- if you won't run away, if you care enough and are willing, and are the only one available, take on this kindly teacher role.

Adults who refuse to accept a rule not to harm others are likely to need incarceration at some point, for some length of time. For you to find out if that is who <u>they</u> are:

Use your good judgment. Calling 911 is a choice, especially if you smell danger has brewed, and you are extremely uncomfortable.

In the meantime, take them on only if you care enough, are willing, and are the best or only one available.

It requires full caring, skills, and a time commitment even by a "professional".

You might remember the accused shooter behind six killings at a Virginia Walmart around thanksgiving 2022, and that he left behind a "death note,": police revealed.

"A few months back I had overheard [REDACTED] talking to [REDACTED] and he told me that he had been trying to get rid of me since day one. After I heard that I lashed out. The associates gave me twisted grins, mocked me and celebrated my down fall the last day. That's why they suffer the same fate as me," Andre Bing, who worked at the Chesapeake Walmart, wrote in his "death note" (pdf) released by Chesapeake Police.

Also in the note, Bing made references to notorious serial killer and cannibal Jeffrey Dahmer. Some co-workers, he wrote, laughed at him "and said that I was like Jeffrey Dahmer ... I would have never killed anyone that entered my home."

Other Walmart associates "gave me evil twisted grins, mocked me and celebrated my down fall (sic) the last day. That's why they will suffer the same fate as me."

Bing also alleged that his "intent was never murder" but "only did it when I realized that my phone was hacked and was giving the worst feeling imaginable."

The note, which included religious references, was redacted slightly to eliminate the names of specific people he mentioned. He also wrote, *My only wish would have been to start over from scratch and that my parents would have paid closer attention to my social deficit.*"

Police revealed Friday that Bing purchased a 9mm handgun on Tuesday morning from a local store hours before he allegedly shot and killed his colleagues. Witnesses told local media that he entered the Walmart break room and opened fire before killing himself.

The six deceased victims were identified as Lorenzo Gamble, Brian Pendleton, Kellie Pyle, Randall Blevins, Tyneka Johnson, and Fernando Jesus Chavez, authorities said. At least six other people were injured in the incident.

What are my reasons for including this homicide/suicide case here?

If YOU had a person in your life similar to this, PRE- homicide/suicide, what would you do?

To me the main sentence in this death note is: "My only wish would have been to start over from scratch and that my parents would have paid closer attention to my social deficit."

If he would have been brought up in your family or in mine, and the system I have described was used with him, it is likely that he would not have gone this far murdering himself and others. Yes, he was a very distressed person, and he needed lots of help at this point. This would be a most difficult case to resolve. Can you see if you would've been his parent or teacher, and in the course of upbringing, would've asked him to take the two rules, would've demonstrated offensiveless defense responses from the get-go, and been the listening for his need of help, as parents, what a difference this would've made by the time he ....let's say started work at Walmart and had the difficulty with colleagues he described?

If no caring and competent professional is available, you may do the next Chapter's plan below.

Chapter 17
System to Help Adults Stop Abusing, and Follow the 2 Rules

First, in your kind parent or teacher tone of voice (as explained above), call out their name(s) to get their attention-- (preferably before much negative has happened, to intervene in the early stages of a problem.)

Then, say that you have a rule not to hurt anybody.

(Demonstrate usually on their wrist to show what that means, if appropriate.

(i.e., "May I put my hand around your wrist?... *See, now YOU can tell that this doesn't hurt. If I went a little harder and harder, it would reach the point of going into hurting* [STOP and RELEASE JUST BEFORE that point.]

"We can both tell the difference- and that's where my rule for myself starts - Not to hurt anybody) And of course if I dug into you -

it would cause pain. You would get angry and want to hurt me back, not trust me, and not want to hear or do what I suggest you do."

*For an emotionally &/or physically abusing parent or spouse, a terrorist or gang member who has been trained to think and value tactics of intimidation, attack, torture, and even assassination to gain control over others, or governments.... Do your best because, yes, you may have placed yourself in harm's way; less so the more a trusted person you are to them.

---You might find it productive to first start here:

You ask, *"Would it be easier for you to not hurt yourself -or easier to not hurt somebody else? (Which rule would be the easiest for you?)"*

a) If it is hardest not to hurt themself: Say, "It seems you haven't taken a rule NOT to hurt yourself (physically, psychologically or both?)" Right? Respectfully and clearly address any and ALL of their objections to taking such a rule not to hurt themself. For example, if they were to say they smoke cigarettes (anything), and drink too much alcohol *"and I'll probably always be that way. I essentially hate myself and constantly put myself down."*

You answer, *"Then are you willing to at least look for solutions for that, and change yourself a step at a time? I can help you with that."* (Listen to their answer(s) and listen for them to say something like, *"If there were a way that I could, I would."*) Remind them that, *"You are worth it, and people who love and like you will be so proud of you as you succeed. You don't have to know how yet, how you need to change; just see the value in taking these rules. Start by taking the rule today that 'I will never again harm myself, and I will keep that rule, day by day. Okay?* Take ALL the time needed to get to "yes, I will". It may take hours for some to come to this conclusion. Do not withhold water, nutritious food, going to the bathroom, and such. Once they have agreed, and see you as a caring helpful person, hold your people accountable. Don't nag; only remind them of their commitment when really necessary. Few enjoy constant repetition.

When they say "yes", see if they will repeat the rule after you. If so, write it down for them.

I am WILLING TO ACCEPT THIS RULE, not to harm myself, as my rule from this moment forward, and I will see how my life goes because of it. "

b) If it is harder not to hurt somebody else:

1. Ask them, *"Tell me the first name of a most difficult person for you not to hurt or to want to harm."*

2. Say, *"You be that person, and I will be you. Tell me a couple of the things they say or do that really gets your 'goat.'"*

3. You stand facing them as they think. You be patient. Have a <u>warm, aware, relaxed, and interested facial ex-</u>

pression, as you look into the pupil of their (usually their right) eye, even if they are looking elsewhere.

--- If it is put-down words and punching, they start to do, tell your adult to show it to you in slow motion. You would circle their wrist with your hand (not hard - just enough for making contact and keep that look as underlined above) while you say an offensiveless defense response such as, "Wow, you're upset with me!....Tell me what I did wrong." Listen to their story and say nothing, OR say, "Tell me more". When they have finished: . Your decisions to hurt and bully others wasn't well thought out from the beginning, or wasn't thought out at all, as being a good plan. You are successful if you can even get them to consider making this shift.

---) You role-play with them your best offensiveless defense responses. Perhaps you'll calmly say, *"I had no idea I was so upsetting to you."* Because YOU are outside of their emotional situation, it will be easier for you to think of how to deliver to them. Since THEY have all the information though, their playing of THAT person will enable YOU to respond to whatever they "throw" at you in a helpful manner*.

Write down a solution that makes sense to them, as they will forget it otherwise. Reassure them that by practicing, it will make the situation easier, also because they have imagined the worst person. They will be appreciative because this is a customized solution based on their input.

If you are quite stymied, I offer you a free Calendly 20 minutes (likely a Zoom call) with me: https://calendly.com/drinafried You're also welcome to have somebody else join us.

To finish: ask again, "NOW ARE YOU WILLING TO AC-CEPT this rule of not harming anyone else, and using Offen-siveless Defense to keep them from harming you without hurting them, as your rule from this moment forward, and never go back?" Take all the time needed to get to "yes".

When they say "yes", see if they will repeat the rule after you. If so, write it down for them.

I am WILLING TO ACCEPT THIS RULE, not to harm others, as my rule from this moment forward, and I will see how my life goes because of it. "

Chapter 18
Your Road to Happiness

Being exponentially more rational, flexible, creative, and using all your available intelligence is your best guide to action.

Say or write a note or letter to your young people. Surely, you will want your and their lives as full as possible of zest, relaxation, purpose, cooperative loving friends and family, with overall rational actions and contentment. Say, "*You will need a roadmap! Here's a good opportunity:*

"*Of course, it's your choice to accept these rules, pass them on, or not take them. However: without BOTH rules, my and your lives will inevitably get worse and worse. You might even topple off a bridge, full of "doom and gloom", sadness, anger, frustration, tension, anxiety, and …pain on some dark emotional days. Hopefully you will be implementing one or more of the systems to release negative emotions safely.*" You may want to review those that are elaborated in Chapter 12.

"*Also, most other people will want revenge if you are harming them; some will do it overtly; some covertly.*

"Here is a positive direction to say in the mirror to yourself: "It's rather simple: I'll just say NO, to all harming of myself and any hurting of others too (physically and psychologically). I'll practice offensiveless defense, and I will say YES to all the other things in the world that make sense and are of interest to me. That's what I am meant to do." Then notice what thoughts come up. *"Find somebody to share what thoughts come up."*

Also notice what <u>feelings</u> arise. If you find you can release feelings easily, do that - while you repeat your positive direction ^ (from above) until you feel confident. Improve on your ^ direction if it brings a shudder or if you laugh, or if tears come- Find your own better direction or perhaps say: *"This is a cinch. I can lead all my (students, children, friends) to take and use these two rules, and learn how to apply offensiveless defense. Easy peasy!"* It may not be true yet, but it is the direction in which you want to go, and by reducing your fear of getting there, you are more likely to get there as long as you continue to use offensiveless defense yourself and persist.

You can do this for yourself. You also can intervene and present this in a timely and compelling way to your friends, students, and family. You can ask, *"Are you willing to take an immutable rule to not to hurt yourself, both physically and not putting your humanness down?*

Can you do this now? You can if you start with the easier people in your life. After you impart this system to a few, you will be more and more ready for people who present more of a challenge. And remember to also ask the equal and outward question, *"Are you willing to take an immutable rule to not to hurt anybody else, both physically and also not putting their humanness down?*

I am here for you, if you need more practice with this blueprint, of what to say, so as to feel comfortable to broach these two rules and offensiveless defense topics to your friends, family, and students. This is what I deal with in my seminars, individual coaching and consulting, and online course. The world will be a better place because of you.

ONE LAST MESSAGE!
CONGRATULATIONS

I am proud of you for making the great decision to interrupt negative patterns in those you care about, including yourself.

You've made your skills better by reading these philosophies and examples. I truly admire and respect you for wanting to improve your life, and the relationships you have. Now it's important to do it, follow the formula and take action each time you see the opportunity- with a smile and confidence. As long as you keep the two rules yourself, and use offensiveless defense when needed, you will be fine.

My mission with this book was to serve you by giving you a system which makes a positive difference in your life; by fast-starting you to think and act differently.

My hope is that you have become more empowered, because of following this recipe to remove negative factors in yourself and in those in your life!

Whether you achieve these dreams and goals is solely up to you. No one can promise or guarantee what level of success you will achieve. You can reach out if you need more help.

Based on research, by following the strategies in this book, YOU CAN influence those around you to live life more fully, by ceasing to harm themselves and others, and to use offensiveless defense to keep yourself and them safe.

Special **FREE** Bonus Gift for You!

To help you achieve more success, there are **FREE BONUS RESOURCES FOR YOU** at:

www.FreeGiftFromDrina.com

- In-depth examples on how you can talk with friends, family, and acquaintances - to help them find a better way, when they are leaning towards harming themselves or hurting somebody else.

- 68 Slide Educational Tool to aid you.

About Drina

Since 2005 Drina has been on a mission to spread the system that only two rules plus offensiveless defense are needed for a happier and safe life. After 32 years as a school psychologist, marriage and family counselor, advisor and coach to parents, teachers, and individuals in all walks of life, Dr. Fried is ready to bring her formula to more, in order to prevent the hardship, anger, fear and sadness that suicide and homicide brings to students, families and friends. The roadmap starts earlier, with the damaging harm introduced before these extremes of homicide and suicide.

Drina's engaging philosophy enables you to fast-start yourself and others' thinking away from psychologically and physically harmful actions. You will be able to fast-start yourself and others to commit to living a life of benefits. Once people learn the formula for offensiveless defense, through their demeanor they will not even be targets of bullies. Sadly, some children are more afraid of talking to their parents than confronting bullies or even committing suicide. However, by using this blueprint, children will appreciate their parents so much that they will be open to talk about anything.

Named School psychologist of the year in Kern County, California she brought her unique blueprint to teachers and parents so they would feel confident and empowered when confronted with stressful situations.

YOU will have the recipe to turn thinking around in order to get back on track to living life the way it was meant to be lived: with delight and possibilities.

Based on research, Drina will be doing online and in-person seminars, mastermind groups, consultations and coaching. You are invited to register for support, tools, resources, training, and continuing education.

www.drinafried.com

Acknowledgments

Throughout my many years, many have shared ideas, mentoring and support that has impacted my life, each in different ways. It's hard to thank everyone, although I think I have. Apologies otherwise. Please know that I appreciate you greatly.

Haim Ginott, deceased author of *"Between Parent and Child"* - fabulous 20th century psychiatrist; Andrew Hangarter for enduring companionship, editing, and counsel; Erik Howard Swanson- for his technical assistance; Cynthia Bledsoe, Mary Lou and Lee Beam, Michael Ciletti, Lily Lambert, Master Amin, Sheryon Pilgrim, Julie Cooley, Lisa James, Sharon Sullivan, Susan Saint-Marie, Julius L. Shaneson, George Golmassian, Marilyn Schanzer Roy, Richard Weinthal, Gayle Rock, Lu Fleming, Margaret Stevens, Christine, Coryn, and JoAn McBride, Heidi and Bob Allison, Valerie Melotti, Julie Winkler, Junko Borge-Harris, Mark Gordon Buckley and Gayle Marie Beckman, Barbara Lent, Linda Detres, Kandy and Tom Sheets, Olga Gault, Robert, Karen, and Brian Sidell, for uplifting my spirits and solving each and every technical problem, and Cathy and Ward Allen-for becoming good and real friends. Sid Simon, Albert Ellis, Mary McCabe, and Harvey Jackins- who led my post-college early psychological journey; Mark Fornasiero and Nicole Hertvik Fornasiero, Mia, Olivia, and Elise Fornasiero, David K. Fried, Hector Fried, Jennifer and Paul Oliver, Amanda and Amber Oliver, Carlotta Fried, Robin, Mirjam, and Kristina Fried, Jeffrey Fried, Talvi Fried, Virginia and John Hertvik, Ray and Sergio Fornasiero, Phyllis Kupferstein, Rebecca and Don Farkas, Robert and Debbie Anton, and Auli Fried- my beloved living real and extended Family. Al Jensen, Judi Moreo, Bruce Merrin, and Ninon de Vere De Rosa- who encouraged me to speak up in my 7th decade; Eileen Maroney and Kathy Hangarter- for keeping track and bookkeeping; Rabbi Gabriel Cousens, MD. Tree of Life Community and Rabbi Johnathan Klein, Temple Beth El, Bakersfield, CA.; Jack Canfield- Author of "Chicken Soup for the Soul" series; Joy Hibbins, author of Suicide Prevention Techniques, Adele Faber & Elaine Mazlish, authors of "How to Talk So Kids Will Listen & Listen So Kids will Talk" and "Siblings Without Rivalry.", Gary Chapman Author of "The Five Love Languages & The Secret to Love That Lasts"; Tony Robbins- Master Entrepreneur, Speaker, Trainer, Consultant and Coach, Dean Grazioso -Entrepreneur and Speaker, Coach Katie, Nick & Megan Unsworth- Founders of "Life on Fire" Programs, and last but not least- James Malinchak, Speaker, Trainer and Consultant who also lives parttime in fabulous Las Vegas.

Bibliography

AARP Bulletin. (November 2022) Task Force Calls for Routine Anxiety Testing. Pg.4

Bennett-Goleman, Tara. (2001). Emotional Alchemy: How the Mind Can Heal the Heart. New York: Harmony.

Drews, Toby Rice. (1980). Getting Them Sober; A guide for those who live with an alcoholic. New Jersey: Bridge Publishing.

The Epoch Times. Virginia Walmart shooter, death note, Nov.2022.

Faber, A. & Mazlish, E.(1980). How to Talk So Kids Will Listen and Listen So Kids Will Talk. New York: Avon Book.

Ginott,Haim. (1965). Between Parent and Child. New York: The Macmillan Company.

Ginott, Haim. (1969). Between Parent and Teenager. New York: The Macmillan Company.

Ginott, Haim. (1972). Teacher and Child. New York: The Macmillan Company.

Glasser, William. (1975). Reality Therapy. New York: Harper & Row.

Goleman, Daniel. (1995). Emotional Intelligence. New York: Bantam Books.

Hibbins, Joy. (2015). Suicide Crisis – The Story. Lulu.com

Hibbins, Joy. (2019). Suicide Prevention Techniques-How A Suicide Crisis Service Saves Lives. Jessica Kingsley publishers; www.jkp.com.

Jackins, Harvey. (1982). Fundamentals of Co-Counseling Manual. Seattle: Rational Island Publishers, p. 43-54.

Jackins, Harvey. (2004). The Human Side of Human Beings. Seattle: Rational Island Publishers. Miller, S., & Dodd, J. (11/23/98)

Rabbitt, Meghan. (2022, Aug.) The Brain Injury Overlooked in Women- Why Women Need to Care About Concussions. Prevention

Made in the USA
Monee, IL
17 March 2023

29839651R00075